The Astrological Kitchen

By: Angela Buck

Tellwell Talent

www.tellwell.ca

ISBN

978-1-77302-618-3 (Hardcover)

978-1-77302-619-0 (Paperback)

Table of Contents

★ ARIES ★
MARCH 21 - APRIL 19
★ THE PIONEER ★

ELEMENT: FIRE
RULING PLANET: MARS
GEMSTONE: DIAMOND

PERSONALITY PROFILE -- ARIES FEMALE

Aries is a fire sign, and you will find plenty of heat in both genders. The Aries female is very enthusiastic, generous and very energetic. This dynamic restlessness will keep both her and those around her on their toes.

Being the first sign on the astral wheel, Aries possesses a pioneering spirit. This can be seen in her approach to life. She is always game to try something new.

The Aries female can be very forthright, making her feelings well known. These women are usually playful, appearing to be fearless, even have a *"devil-may-care"* attitude toward life. They enjoy very physical activities such as skiing, soccer and tennis. These females are often sport fans, very able to join the male crowd huddled around the big screen around World Cup or Super Bowl time. This woman can be found tailgating on any given Sunday.

She is lively, generous, enterprising, and passionate about life; her strong air of independence and incurably romantic spirit leave much to be admired.

When it comes to the home of the Aries female, the visitor will be struck by its informal charm. This is usually because she is rarely ever there, or has been up working all night. She feels she has better things to do than bore herself with menial housework. If the choice is the mop or going out with friends, guess which one she will choose? One should note that this woman views her home as an extension of herself, and it is quite possible that you will see her own paintings decorating the walls or drinking her morning cup of joe out of a mug that she molded in pottery class. Her avant garde spirit can also be present in her taste of clothing – she loves new designers and is always on trend!

PERSONALITY PROFILE -- ARIES MALE

The Aries male is original, energetic and restless -- he *rams his* way through life. Being imaginative and dynamic positively counteracts being impractical and impulsive. He makes things happen, and this equates for exciting company! This man is very freedom loving and is **not** interested in conventional rules and traditions.

He can give the "impression" of selfishness -- usually putting himself first, and wanting everything **now**. Although he appears to be selfish, he will give everything he has to the object to his affection…whether it be a sweetheart, his friends or his children. When this man loves, he lets it be known. They are ardent suitors.

The Aries man can have a fine sense of humor, and enjoys his company to be intelligent as well as physically attractive. He is clever at repartee, and can be thought of as quite the satirist, so stay on your toes and be prepared to laugh.

If there is any spare time, the Arian will find a physical outlet for his intense energy in robust sports such as hockey, football, or boxing. As he ages he will be an avid spectator of sports and maybe cast a wager on a game here or there. His love of sports is reflected in his home decor. His skates are at the door, his golf clubs are likely to take the place of an end table, and his surfboard may double as a coffee table. Don't be surprised to find remote control cars and drones in this man's garage, or a Go Pro securely fastened to his helmet ready for a day of mountain bike riding or sky diving!

This is a man who demands action, risk, and excitement in his life. Fortunately, he gives lots back.

FAMOUS ARIES

Reese Witherspoon	Danica Patrick
Keira Knightley	Sophia Benito
Robert Downey Jr.	Ewan McGregor
Rosie Huntington-Whiteley	Jennifer Garner
Michael Fassbender	Scott Eastwood
Russell Crowe	Marlon Brando
Alec Baldwin	Nathan Fillion
Jackie Chan	Pharrell Williams

HERBS AND FOODS ASSOCIATED WITH ARIES

Leeks
Onion
Shallot
Capers
Mustard
Cayenne
Pepper Red
Chili
Peppermint
Lamb

FLOWERS AND PLANTS

Honeysuckle
Thistle
Bryony
Hops

AROMATHERAPY

Peppermint, Rosemary, Cinnamon

SET THE TABLE & BRING THE WINE

As you have well gathered by now, entertaining Aries individuals successfully demands quick types of foods, as they are eager and want everything on the spot. These attributes lend themselves to having a ready and varied supply of appetizers to take the edge off the raw hunger and leave yourself time to prepare the entree. BBQ is a favorite form of an Arian meal, and he or she will often volunteer to wield the grilling tools, as they enjoy this activity. It helps sate their restlessness and keeps them busy.

Arians love spicy foods, so don't spare the peppers, cayenne or curry. Never to be left behind, Aries love foods that are on the cutting edge; they are not afraid to experiment. They have a preference for lively, robust dishes, which reflect their progressive spirit.

The Arian is not a typical one- on -one dinner partner. These people are outgoing and gregarious, preferring a plenitude of other guests who share their *joie de vivre.*

The dinner should be informal; if it's a dinner party, keep the table setting tastefully underdone – nothing frilly and no doilies PLEASE! If it is a dinner of a romantic nature, set the table with some fragrant red roses, stems cut short so you can see each other from across the table. Aries signature color is red!! Also, adorn the table and room with some candles, dim the lights but not too low…they like light. A great way to entertain Aries is to set up a self serve bar, replete with a bucket of ice, a variety of different glasses, spirits, and mix. Don't forget a bucket full of cold beer! Aries will love the ease of being able to mix their own drink, (and everyone else's). They make fabulous bartenders. Along side of the bar, you should have your appetizers present…keep them hip, none of your grandma's devilled eggs here. Aries wants current, cutting edge food. Whatever you choose to serve, make sure there is some heat…..sriracha comes to mind. Also, if you're running short on time, or it's an impromptu gathering (which with Aries is VERY common), chips with salsa is a sure bet every time.

They love noise! To compliment the lively discussion at your dinner party, a good suggestion would be music that is upbeat. They love up and coming artists, so you might want to play some new Indie bands or the Alternative Rock station on your digital radio.

Here are some menu plans that are sure to perk up the ears of your Arian guests.

Who doesn't like good huevos rancheros? Your Aries certainly will! This dish is perfect for brunch, lunch or even dinner. Serve with *mango margaritas*, or if your guest doesn't drink, a yummy *mango ice* will cool the

Huevos Rancheros

(1 tbsp) olive oil

1 medium red or yellow pepper seeded and cut into 1/4" pieces

2 medium tomatoes, seeded and cut into 1/2" pieces

1 cup bottled or homemade salsa

1/3 cup drained, pickled green chili peppers

½ tsp. ground cumin

1 cup spicy, black beans (recipe to follow)

6 large eggs

¼ cup crumbled cotija cheese

6 large flour or corn tortillas, warmed

2 tbsp chopped cilantro

1 avocado, pitted, peeled and chopped

Heat oil in a medium frying pan over medium heat. Add pepper; sauté until slightly softened, about three minutes. Add tomato, salsa, chili peppers and cumin. Simmer for 7 to 10 minutes, until thickened.

Crack eggs onto sauce without breaking yolks; top with cheese. Cook, covered, until whites are set, three to five minutes.

To serve, place an egg with sauce and spicy black beans on top of each tortilla. Sprinkle with cilantro and avocado.

Spicy Black Beans

2 tsp. canola oil

1 small jalapeño pepper; seeded and minced

½ small onion; minced

1 clove garlic; minced

1 15 oz. can black beans; rinsed

In a medium skillet heat oil. Add pepper & onion and sauté until onions are soft; about 3 minutes. Add garlic and beans and cook until beans are warmed through. Season with salt and pepper and remove from heat.

Mango Ice

4 ripe mangoes (about 3 1/2 pounds total)

1 cup simple syrup

3 tablespoons fresh lime juice, or to taste

Fresh mint springs for garnish

Wash and dry mangoes. Using a sharp knife, remove the 2 flat sides of each mango, cutting lengthwise alongside pit and cutting as close to pit as possible so that mango flesh is in 2 large pieces. With a spoon carefully scoop flesh from mango sides into a blender. With a knife cut remaining flesh from pit and add to blender. Add syrup and lime juice to blender and purée until smooth. Put in a metal bowl and freeze for at least 8 hours.. You can make this up to a week ahead. Scoop into pretty serving dishes and garnish with fresh mint sprigs.

Rack of Lamb w/ Mustard Crust

2 racks (8ribs each) of lamb

1 tsp. sea salt

3 tsp. freshly ground black pepper

3 tsp. fresh rosemary

1/8 cup canola oil

¼ cup grainy mustard

½ cup bread crumbs

Preheat oven to 400°.

In a large, heavy skillet, heat oil until hot, not smoking. Rub rosemary, salt and pepper evenly over lamb racks. Brown all sides of meat in skillet.

Place meat, fat side up on a baking dish and cook in oven until the internal temperature of meat is 145°. Remove from oven and let rest for about 3 minutes. Brush mustard evenly over meat. Place breadcrumbs on a large plate. Carefully lift meat with a pair of tongs and roll mustard covered lamb in breadcrumbs until evenly coated. Return to oven and bake for another 7 – 10 minutes until golden brown.

Remove from oven and let meat rest for about 5 minutes. Cut into chops and serve immediately.

Spicy Green Beans

2 cups green or wax beans; snipped and cleaned

1 shallot; thinly sliced

1 tbsp. mustard seeds

2 tbsp. olive oil

2 tbsp. butter

Salt & pepper to taste

Capers are a misunderstood ingredient. Is it seafood, is it a vegetable? Nope. It's actually a flower bud. Capers come from the Mediterranean bush, capparis spinosa. Before the bush flowers, the "bud" is picked and pickled. Yes, it is technically a flower bud. These small buds pack a lot of punch. Add a couple of them to any dish that needs a bit of livening up. Aries love them!

Heat a skillet over medium-high heat until pan is hot. Add mustard seeds and move them around constantly with a wooden spatula. Be careful not to burn them. When the seeds start to "*pop*", add the oil, butter, shallot, beans, salt and pepper. Reduce heat to medium and sauté until cooked, but firm, about 4 minutes. Enjoy.

Chicken Picatta

4 - 4oz. chicken breasts

1 tsp. sea salt

1 tsp. black pepper

½ cup all purpose flour for dredging

¼ cup canola oil

1 clove garlic; minced

1 tbsp. fresh lemon juice

¼ cup white wine (you can use chicken stock)

1 tbsp. nonpareil capers

2 tbsp. butter; chilled

2 tbsp. minced parsley

Lemon slices for garnish

Season chicken breast with salt and pepper. Dredge each breast in flour; shaking off any excess flour. Heat oil in a heavy skillet. Sauté the chicken breasts until golden brown and cooked all the way through; about 7 minutes. Transfer chicken to a serving platter. Return pan to medium high heat. Add lemon juice and wine, being sure to scrape the bottom of the pan with a wooden spatula (this will release the flavor from the chicken). Add capers and cook for another 30 seconds. Remove pan from heat and whisk in butter until sauce is smooth and velvety; about 30 seconds. Garnish with parsley and lemon slices. Serve with smashed potatoes and caramelized onions. This is really delicious!

Garlic Smashed Potatoes

4 large white potatoes

¼ cup whole milk; warmed in microwave for 3o seconds

2 tbsp. salted butter

1 clove garlic; minced

Salt and pepper to taste

Peel and cut potatoes in quarters. Add to a pot of cold water and boil until tender. About 15 minutes. Drain water and return pot to medium low heat. Add warm milk, butter and garlic and "smash" potatoes with a fork. The potatoes should be a little chunky. Season with salt and pepper.

Caramelized Onions

1 large red onion; sliced

2 tsp. olive oil

2 tsp. butter

1 tsp. brown sugar

Salt & pepper to taste

Heat oil and butter in a large, heavy skillet over medium heat and sauté onions until they begin to lose their moisture. When onions begin to brown add sugar and continue to cook until they are browned. Remove from heat and season with salt and pepper.

Leek, Onion & Bacon Quiche

CRUST

2 ½ cups of flour

¼ tsp. salt

1 ½ sticks of cold, unsalted butter

1 egg yolk

¼ + 2 tbsp. ice water

½ tsp. vinegar

Make the crust. In a food processor, pulse the 2 1/2 cups of flour with the salt. Add the butter and pulse until it is the size of small peas. Add the egg yolk, vinegar and ice water. Pulse until the pastry is moistened. Turn the pastry out onto a floured work surface and knead 2 or 3 times, just until smooth. Pat the pastry into 2 disks, wrap in plastic, and refrigerate until firm, about 20 minutes.

Preheat the oven to 375 degrees. On a floured surface, roll out both disks of the pastry to a 12-inch rounds. Ease the pastry into a 10-inch fluted tart pan Trim any excess and use it to patch any holes. Refrigerate the tart shells for 10 minutes.

Line the tart shells with foil and fill with pie weights or dried beans. Bake the tart shells for 30 minutes, just until dry. Remove the foil and pie weights and bake the crusts for about 15 minutes longer, until they are dry and golden. Transfer the tart pans to two baking sheets.

1 pound thick bacon or pancetta; diced

3 leeks; cleaned and white and light green part diced

1 tsp. fresh thyme

Dash of nutmeg

½ tsp. red pepper flakes

6 large eggs

2 cups heavy cream

Salt and pepper to taste

2 cups Gruyere cheese; grated

In a large skillet, cook the bacon over moderately high heat, stirring, until browned and crisp, about 7 minutes. Drain all but 1 tablespoon of the fat in the pan. Add the leeks, nutmeg, pepper flakes and thyme to bacon, season with salt and pepper, and cook over moderate heat, stirring occasionally, until the leeks are softened but not browned, about 5 minutes. Transfer to a bowl and let cool. Whisk eggs and heavy cream in a bowl. Stir in the bacon mixture and cheese.

Divide evenly between the two pans and bake until cooked through and begins to brown; about 35 minutes. Remove from oven and let cool before serving; about 20 minutes. Serve with the frissee salad.

Frissee Salad w/ Curried Vinaigrette

1 lb. frissee lettuce; cleaned and roughly torn

3 radish; cleaned and sliced very thin

½ cup extra virgin olive oil

¼ cup red wine vinegar

2 shallots; minced

1 small, red chili pepper; seed and minced

1 tsp. mild or hot curry powder

1 tsp. brown sugar

Salt and pepper to taste

In a large salad bowl, combine lettuce and radish. In a separate bowl, whisk together remaining ingredients. Drizzle over salad and toss well. Enjoy this simple, yet flavorful salad.

★ TAURUS ★
APRIL 21 - MAY 21
★ THE STABILIZER ★

ELEMENT: EARTH
RULING PLANET: VENUS
GEMSTONE: EMERALD

PERSONAL PROFILE -- TAURUS FEMALE

Taurus is an earth sign; thus, the female Taurean will be earthy and sensuous. In business and family affairs, she can be practical, patient and reliable. In romantic arenas, she is quite sentimental and easily becomes attached. This woman knows what she wants, and will go to great lengths to achieve it. She is very determined. Her powers of endurance are noteworthy. She is intuitively intelligent.

The Taurean woman dresses tastefully, but not lavishly. She knows how to work within the guidelines of a budget, and to get the most bang for her buck. She appreciates luxury, and adores jewelry, especially necklaces.

This woman may appear vulnerable, but don't fool yourself, she is not! She is constantly stubborn and persistent, which allows her to weather many rough storms. She makes a steadfast friend who will stick with you through thick and thin. She always has a strong shoulder to lean on.

The Taurean woman's home will be cozy and comfortable. Hearth and home are her middle names, and she will structure her world around it. Whereas the more outgoing signs prefer a night on the town, this female opts for a warm night in front of the fire; the noise of the city is not for her. Give her the quiet of the countryside any day. Her home will probably be rich in woodwork, and these brown hues will be complimented by greens and blues.

This is an all-rounded woman. She has a love of beauty and the arts, and may well possess a pleasing singing voice of her own.

Taurus is ruled by the throat; many famous singers fall under this sign. She has a wholesome, practical outlook on life, and an intuitive grasp on what is right for her.

PERSONAL PROFILE -- TAURUS MALE

To represent the Taurean male, we will put forth the metaphor of the strong, sturdy oak tree, having deep roots imbedded in the soil. This man is reliable, and someone you can always count on. Once his mind is made up, don't bother confusing him with the facts.

A feeling of security is vital to him: he will demand it in his career, his home life, and his marriage. He is generally very patient with life's ups and downs and generally takes everything in stride.

Mainly he will exude an abundance of warmth, charm, and affection. He will refuse to be pushed or rushed. Risk-taking is for the Aries or Scorpio individual -- not for The Bull. He is conservative and weights things heavily before making a decision; but once a decision is made, he will honor it.

He has a wonderful business sense and is generally good with money and investments. This man feels right at home working in a bank or real estate. He usually owns his own home early in life and acquisitions are of great consequence to him--whether it be real estate, art, or luxury items for the home. **Things** count strongly and add to their security and well being. Of course he would rather have his proud possessions displayed in a country manner than an urban condo.

Health wise, this man has an extremely strong constitution and longevity is associated with this sign. He loves good food and appreciates a fine wine.

In this case, the way to this man's heart is definitely through his stomach. And that's no *bull*.

FAMOUS TAUREANS

Channing Tatum	Dwayne Johnson
Kelly Clarkson	Megan Fox
George Clooney	Barbara Streisand
Cate Blanchet	Al Pacino
Adele	Billy Joel
Jack Nicolson	John Cena
Jerry Seinfeld	Salvatore Dali

HERBS AND FOODS ASSOCIATED WITH TAURUS

Any type of meat	Asparagus
Pears	Apples
Artichoke	Grapes
Figs	Wheat
Cloves	Sorrel

FLOWERS AND PLANTS

Crab Apple	Cypress
Rose	Violet
Foxglove	Daisy
Poppy	Columbine

AROMATHERAPY

Eucalyptus, apple blossom, spearmint

SET THE TABLE AND BRING THE WINE

No plastic flowers please, when entertaining Taureans. Fresh flowers for the centerpiece on your dining table would be more appropriate and appealing. The colors of the bouquet should be in soft pinks, light blues and pale greens. In warm weather, dining al fresco while eating on the patio with flower and vegetable gardens in sight, make for the optimum setting. The dinner should be of substance….good earthen ware or weighty ceramic dishes are a good choice. If you are serving a stew or casserole, I suggest you serve it out of the Dutch oven you used to bake it in. …..they love oven to table dishes. Also, they love bread, so don't forget to have a whole baguette or loaf on the table. Have the whole loaf on a wooden cutting board with a bread knife and real butter. They will delight in cutting the bread themselves or even better, *breaking bread* with their hands.

The aroma of good cooking and the bouquet of fine wine will get you everywhere with people born under this sign. Significant to these people is the savoring of sauces and gravies. The portions should be generous, for Taurus has a formidable appetite. Taureans relish a hearty, home cooked dinner that shows you made a special effort to please. As previously mentioned, the old adage that the way to a person's heart is through the stomach was probably written for people born under this sign.

Keep this in mind when entertaining Taurus individuals -- while they delight in excellent food and fine wine, they like to see money well spent. It would be best to not be needlessly extravagant, because the Taurean will be aware of, and respect the fact that you were attempting to be careful with your dollar. It needn't be a Beef Wellington; a delectable beef stew or pot roast will suffice.

It has the ring of a satisfying evening --the product of your hard work will be --gone! If you do happen to have any leftovers, pack them in a container to go. While your Taurean friend is eating it later, and they will, they will be thinking of you!!!

Following are some hearty menu plans worthy of your Taurean guests.

Braised Beef Shanks In Red Wine

over Buttery Mashed Potatoes

¼ cup canola oil

4 large "soup cut" beef shanks

Salt and pepper to taste

1 large onion; diced

1 carrot; peeled and diced

1 lb. mushrooms; preferably button & cremini

2 tsp. fresh thyme

1 tsp. fresh rosemary

½ tsp. red pepper flakes

2 cloves garlic; minced

2 cups red wine

¼ cup Port

3 tbsp. tomato paste

1 cup beef stock

In a large, heavy Dutch oven heat oil until very hot. Season shanks on both sides with salt and pepper. Add shanks and brown on both sides; about 6 minutes. Remove meat to plate. Add onion, carrot and mushrooms to pan and sauté for about 3 minutes. Add thyme, rosemary, pepper flakes and garlic. Sauté for another minute. Add red wine and port and scrape bottom of pan with a wooden spoon while bringing mixture to a low boil. Stir in tomato paste and beef stock and bring to a boil.

Add beef shanks and juices back to the pot, cover with lid and reduce heat. Simmer on low for 3 1/2 hours or until shank is tender.

Serve shanks over buttery mashed potatoes and ladle sauce over top. Your Taurus is going to LOVE this dish. Don't forget to serve some crunchy bread on the side.

Poached Pears

4 ripe pears; Bartlet or Bosc

1 cup sweet, red wine

¾ cup sugar

1 cinnamon stick

1 vanilla bean

4 cloves

1 orange peel

Water

Peel pears, being very careful not to remove the stem. Mix together wine and sugar. Arrange pears in a deep saucepan. Pour wine mixture over pears and arrange cinnamon, vanilla bean, cloves and orange peel in pot. Add enough water so that pears are totally covered in liquid. Bring pears to a gentle boil over medium heat,. Simmer until pears are tender; about 15 minutes. Remove from heat and let pears cool in pot in their own liquid. When pears are cooled, remove to a serving dish. Strain liquid and discard the cinnamon etc. Bring liquid back to a gentle boil and reduce by half; about 45 minutes. The liquid should be syrupy.

Spoon liquid over pears and serve with vanilla ice cream.

Although most Taureans are carnivores, there are a few vegetarian bulls out there. These next few recipes are for them. Although they are meatless recipes, they are still hearty.

Mushroom & Sorrel Papparadelle

12 oz. dried pappardelle pasta

½ tsp. salt

½ stick of salted butter 2

tbsp. olive oil

1 lb. of mushrooms; such as button, oyster or cremini; sliced

1 cup cleaned sorrel leaves, torn

Pinch of nutmeg

½ cup of white wine 6 oz.

brie cheese

Salt and pepper to taste

¼ cup of grated parmesan

Bring a pot of salted water to a boil. Cook pasta until al dente; about 8 minutes. Drain pasta and reserve about ¼ cup of cooking water.
In a large skillet heat olive oil and butter, add mushrooms in batches until brown. Add sorrel and cook slightly; about 1 minute. Add garlic, nutmeg, stir. Add wine and cook until wine is reduced by half; about 3 minutes. Add brie, pasta and a little of the cooking liquid. Season with salt and pepper. Toss pasta until cheese begins to melt. Turn onto serving platter and sprinkle with grated parmesan. Mmmm, so yummy.

The Astrological Kitchen by Angela Buck

Many people miss out on the wonderful experience of eating artichokes simply because they are intimidated by this prickly vegetable. Don't be! Artichokes are surprisingly simple to prepare and chock full of dietary fiber, magnesium and vitamin C!

Baked Artichokes

3 large artichokes

2 tbsp. fresh rosemary

2 tsp. fresh lemon juice

1 stick salted butter

sea salt and pepper to taste

2 tbp. torn parsley for garnish

Preheat oven to 425°.

Trim stem and tip of each artichoke. Next, trim the outer leaves; this can easily be done with a pair of kitchen scissors. Cut artichokes in half lengthwise. Place 6 pieces of artichokes in large baking dish.

Mix remaining ingredients together in small bowl. Spread half of the butter mixture evenly over artichokes. Cover with foil and bake for 45 minutes. Remove foil and continue to bake for 10 minutes, or until golden brown. Remove from oven and spread the remaining butter mixture over artichokes and garnish with fresh parsley. Serve immediately. See, wasn't that easy?

Hot Apple Crumb

Hot Apple Crumb

Filling

3 1/4 pounds Granny Smith apples, peeled, cored, sliced 1/4
inch thick

2/3 cup sugar

2 tablespoons all purpose flour

2 teaspoons ground cinnamon

2 tablespoons unsalted butter, melted

Topping

1 cup all purpose flour

1/2 cup sugar

1/2 cup (packed) golden brown sugar

1 1/2 teaspoons ground cinnamon

1/2 teaspoon salt

6 tablespoons chilled unsalted butter, cut into 1/2-inch cubes

For filling:

Mix all ingredients in large bowl to coat apples.

For topping:

Blend first 5 ingredients in processor. Add chilled butter cubes; using the pulse button, mix until mixture is a coarse grain.

Preheat oven to 375°. Toss filling and transfer to buttered baking dish. Pack topping over and around apples. Bake pie on baking sheet until topping is golden, about 40 minutes (cover top with foil if browning too quickly). Reduce oven temperature to 350°F. Bake until apples in center are tender when pierced and filling is bubbling at edges, about 45 minutes longer. Cool until warm, about 1 hour. Serve with ice cream.

Chicken & Vegetable Pot Pie

4 pounds chicken breasts with skin and bones

6 cups low-salt chicken broth

½ cup frozen peas

3 large carrots, peeled, cut into 1/2-inch pieces

1 pound turnips, peeled, cut into 1/2-inch pieces

2 medium potatoes: peeled cut into ½ -pieces

1/4 cup (1/2 stick) butter

3 medium leeks (white and pale green parts only), sliced

2 large shallots, minced

2 tablespoons minced fresh thyme

1 tsp. fresh minced rosemary

1/2 cup all purpose flour

1/2 cup dry white wine

1/2 cup whipping cream

pinch of nutmeg

Salt & pepper to taste

1 tbsp. butter (for greasing the ramekins)

1 package phyllo dough

3 tbsp. melted butter

Place chicken breasts in heavy large pot. Add just enough broth to cover chicken. Bring broth to boil; reduce heat to low. Cover pot and simmer until chicken is just cooked through, skimming surface occasionally, about 20 minutes. Using tongs, transfer chicken to plate and cool.

Add carrots, turnips & potatoes to chicken broth in pot. Simmer uncovered until vegetables are just tender, about 10 minutes. Using slotted spoon, transfer vegetables to large mixing bowl. Add frozen peas. Strain broth; reserve 4 cups. Remove skin and bones from chicken. Cut meat into 1/2- to 3/4-inch pieces. Add chicken to vegetables and stir. Melt butter in same pot over medium heat. Add leeks, shallots, rosemary and thyme. Sauté until tender, about 8 minutes. Add flour and stir 2 minutes. Stir in 4 cups broth and white wine. Increase heat and bring to boil, stirring constantly. Reduce heat and add cream, simmer until sauce thickens enough to coat spoon, whisking frequently, about 6 minutes. Season with nutmeg, salt and pepper. Pour gravy over chicken & vegetable mixture. Stir to blend. Cool 45 minutes. (Filling can be made 1 day ahead. Cover and refrigerate.)

Preheat oven to 400°F.

Generously butter 6 individual ramekins. Evenly add chicken mixture to each ramekin; about ¾ full.

Roll out crust dough. Place a pastry sheet round on top of your pot pies and make a slit in the middle of the crust with the back of your knife. Place ramekins on baking sheet and bake until crust is golden and gravy is bubbling, about 30 minutes. Let stand 10 minutes before serving.

Sorrel, Apple & Walnut Salad

1 large bunch sorrel; cleaned and torn

1 green apple; cored and sliced

1 handful of walnuts (optional)

Place all ingredients in a salad bowl and toss together with vinaigrette.

1 cup extra virgin olive oil

¼ cup red wine vinegar

½ tsp. Dijon mustard

Salt & pepper to taste

Whisk together all ingredients

★ GEMINI ★

MAY 21 - JUNE 20
★ THE COMMUNICATOR ★

ELEMENT: AIR
RULING PLANET: MERCURY
GEMSTONE: AGATE / ALEXANDRITE

This is the most youthful of all the signs, so this female will appear ageless. She is the envy of all the other signs.

The Gemini woman is an air sign, which gives her a strong urge to communicate. She can get and maintain almost anyone's attention, for she is a delightful conversationalist, witty and charming. She can also be a compassionate listener, so you can let go with your desires and fears, and receive some insightful responses. Gemini doesn't mind getting involved in others peoples' circumstances; they love to analyze situations and tender advice.

Friends are made easily, but this woman prefers to keep relationships on a light basis, rather than on a long term, more demanding one. She is more inclined to the occasional phone call or text than to the intensity of a daily one on one. This woman is affectionate and genial. Popularity is high on her scale and she will have many acquaintances from many walks of life. A real social butterfly.

Many outlets are required to satisfy her abundant energy. She is hard pressed to finish one project before beginning the next: the temptation of something new to challenge her intellect and curiosity can be overwhelming!

Because of this woman's complexity, she often feels disorganized. Losing keys, sunglasses, and other personal items is common for the female Gemini. Her mind is always on something else.

She makes a wonderful go between because she is inclined to depend on intelligence rather than emotion when looking for a solution to a problem. Gemini is ruled by Mercury. This planet rules the psyche; therefore, you must aspire to meet her intellectual standards when trying to get your point across. Tears and drama don't work with this woman, just the facts please.

She is forever experimenting with new ideas in all areas: food, diets, interior decorating; you name it! Because of this, entertaining your Gemini guest will always be a mix of creative and imaginative. Change is her one & only constant. It is recommended to ask this woman what new food trends she is following…this will be your barometer for what to serve at dinner.

This woman views her home as a kind of launching pad from which her other activities will flow. The typical Gemini woman's abode can easily get in to a bit of disarray. One thing you can count on is that there will be several well-stocked book shelves, for books and words are a large part of her persona. You could also find a stack of Sudoku or crossword puzzles on her end table, a *mixed bag* of e-books on her Kindle and a plethora of apps on her ever-present smart phone. She finds everything fascinating!

She may be hard to keep up with, but she will always keep you interested!

PERSONAL PROFILE -- GEMINI MALE

This man is always on the move. Like his female counterpart, he is curious and always seeking new ideas and information. No matter what he is doing at the moment, he is always thinking of the next step.

The Gemini male is unusually intelligent and has what is commonly referred to as the *gift-of-gab*. He loves to talk, and will glibly go from subject to subject, while the rattled listener gets dizzy from trying to keep up.

He enjoys getting a brilliant idea off the ground, then allocating the details to others. Like his fellow air sign, Aquarius, Geminis are capable of turning these creative notions into profitable inventions. They have a spark of genius and Voilla! they have just come up with the next big thing! These men also make wonderful advertising executives…they are always on the cutting edge of what is trending. Of all the signs, Gemini is by far the consummate dilettante, knowing a little bit about everything, never satiating his incurable curiosity about life. He is adaptable and versatile in any situation.

This man's home will reflect his inquisitive spirit…you may find a telescope poised in front of his balcony window, chess board set up in the corner and a stack of magazines on his coffee table. He wants to know a little about EVERYTHING!

This is a vital and interesting man, who seems to have captured the essence and zest for life. He has perfected the art of staying young. This Peter Pan never seems to grow old. Good for him!

FAMOUS GEMINIS

Donald Trump

Angelina Jolie

Nicole Kidman

Collin Ferrell

Liam Neeson

Mark Wahlberg

Prince

Natalie Portman

Johnny Depp

Mary-Kate & Ashley Olsen

Prince William

Brooke Shields

Kanye West

Miles Davis

HERBS AND FOODS ASSOCIATED WITH GEMINI

Chicken

Broad Beans

Aniseed

Caraway

Aniseed

Peas

Lettuce

Nuts

Edaname

Marjoram

Chestnut

Basil

Fish

Sprouts

FLOWERS AND PLANTS

Lavender

Maidenhair

Fern

Lily of the Valley

Myrtle

AROMATHERAPY

Bergamot, basil, lavender

SET THE TABLE AND BRING THE WINE

It is almost impossible for the Gemini to peruse a restaurant menu and quickly decide what to order. Invariably, a small groan is uttered, with the words "I'd like a bit of everything".

Keep this in mind when planning your dinner party. Also to consider is the fact that all the Air signs are fairly light eaters, so the hearty beef stew that so enticed the Taurean, would not have the same positive effect on the Gemini. Any new and unusual dishes or new trending food movements should also be considered when entertaining this duplicitous sign. Like I wrote in the Gemini Female profile, it is wise to ask your Gemini guest (male & female) what new food trends they are following. They are ALWAYS changing their diets and food preferences. This comes in handy when planning your party.

Keep the atmosphere light, with a touch of whimsy for this sign. Adorn the table with hues of yellow, this could include gold, canary yellow, even mustard yellow. Accent colors should include white and lavender. Keep a variety of condiments present on your table, especially non conventional ones.....remember, they are driven by their curiosity. The music can be any genre, as long as it's interesting....no boring elevator type music here! You should suggest to your Gemini guest if THEY would like to choose the dinner music, they'll be happy to oblige.

Remember how inquisitive these people are. A fondue would satisfy all the requirements of assortment, interest, and light dining. It also lends itself to congenial conversation, which is, after all, what really satisfies any Gemini individual. A colorful, artistically arranged seafood platter, a mixed grill, or combination vegetable kabobs would also gratify the need for variety, and for these people, variety is indeed the spice of life. Gemini hates schedules, so it is best to not set an exact time for your party to commence. It's better to say sixish rather than promptly at six. They are not prisoners to the clock.

It is optimum if you can involve two Gemini people in any party, because then you will not have to worry about it being a success. Gemini won't allow the group to slide off into apathy, because that would mean **they** would be bored, and that is unacceptable! Introduce Gemini to your *shy* friend who needs that special person to bring out their best qualities. Let Gemini do the talking. They are spontaneous, self-starters, and you will find yourself inviting these vibrant, magnetic people back again and again.

Here are some imaginative menu plans for your Gemini guests.

Fondue in Three Pots

OIL POT

Peanut Oil

Heat oil to 325°degrees in a

stainless steel or cast iron

fondue pot

To Dip:

Meat cut into cubes about

3/4" (beef, pork, chicken,

scallops)

Vegetables - Broccoli, Cauliflower, Bell

Peppers, mushrooms etc.

Cubes of crunchy French or Italian bread

PEANUT ALERT!!
This recipe calls for peanut oil, because this oil has a higher smoking point. This means it is great for deep frying, but not so great if you have a peanut allergy! Please, make sure no one at your fondue party has a peanut allergy. If you are unsure, use good quality canola oil.

Getting the cheese to the right consistency in a fondue can be a little tricky. To avoid a big, ball of cheese, make sure to stir the cheese in a zig zag pattern when melting. If you stir the cheese in a circular pattern it will "ball up". Now go ahead, fire up the lava lamp and enjoy your fondue party!

CHEESE POT

1 garlic clove, halved crosswise

1 1/2 cups dry white wine (preferably Swiss, such as Fendant)

1 tablespoon cornstarch

2 teaspoons Kirsch (a liqueur found in any liquor store)

2 cups Emmental cheese, coarsely grated

2 cups Gruyere, coarsely grated freshly ground pepper

Pinch of nutmeg

Freshly ground pepper

long wooden skewers

Rub inside of a 4-quart heavy pot with cut sides of garlic, then discard garlic. Add wine to pot and bring just to a simmer over moderate heat.

Whisk together cornstarch and Kirsch in a cup.

Gradually add cheese to pot and cook, stirring constantly in a zigzag pattern (not a circular motion) to prevent cheese from balling up, until cheese is just melted and creamy (do not let boil). Stir cornstarch mixture again and stir into cheese. Bring cheese to a simmer, stirring, until thickened; 5 to 8 minutes.

Season with freshly, ground pepper and nutmeg.

Transfer to fondue pot set over a flame and serve with bread for

dipping.

CHOCOLATE POT

1 15-ounce can sweetened cream of coconut (such as Coco
Lopez)
12 ounces bittersweet (not unsweetened) or semisweet
chocolate, finely chopped
1/4 cup whipping cream
1/4 teaspoon coconut extract
Assorted fresh fruit (such as whole strawberries, 1-inch-thick
slices banana, 1-inch cubes peeled cored pineapple)
Marshmallows for dipping
Pieces of biscotti for dipping

Combine sweetened cream of coconut and 12 ounces chocolate
in heavy large saucepan. Stir mixture over very low heat until
chocolate melts and mixture is smooth. Stir in whipping cream
and extract. (Fondue can be prepared 8 hours ahead. Cover;
store at room temperature. Stir over low heat to warm before
serving.)

Transfer mixture to fondue pot. Place over candle or canned heat burner. Serve with fruit, marshmallows & biscotti. Don't forget the coffee!

It is very important not to use a poor quality wine when cooking this dish or any other. Quality wine does not have to be expensive; there are many great tasting wines that do not break the bank. Ask an associate at your local wine store for some great finds.

Clams & Sausage Over Linguine

2 sweet Italian sausage: crumbled

¼ cup olive oil

2 tbsp. unsalted butter

2 cloves garlic: minced

12 littleneck clams: cleaned

¼ cup dry white wine

¼ cup chicken stock

2 cups cooked linguine

3 tbsp. fresh parsley: minced

¼ cup fresh Romano cheese: grated

In a large skillet, heat oil and sauté sausage until brown, about 5 minutes. Add butter and garlic and cook for about 1 minute. Add clams, wine and stock. Bring to a boil and cook until clams open (discard any clams that do not open). Add pasta (and a little pasta water) and toss until well incorporated. Transfer to a serving platter and sprinkle parsley and cheese on top. Delicious!

The secret to a really good Mussels Fra Diavolo is the red sauce. Take your time and make your own. Make a double batch and put some in the freezer for later. This sauce is so versatile; you can put it on seafood, pasta or mix it with vegetables for a quick, meatless lunch.

Mussels Fra Diavolo

Red Sauce

3 tbsp. canola oil

1 medium onion; diced

2 carrots; peeled & diced

1 tsp. red pepper flakes

1 tsp. oregano

1 tsp. basil

4 cloves garlic; minced

1 cup red wine

2 15oz. cans Italian, plum tomatoes; crushed

2 tbsp. tomato paste

Salt & pepper to taste

In large, heavy pot heat oil until hot. Add onion and carrots and sauté until soft; about 5 minutes. Add red pepper, oregano, basil and garlic and stir. Add red wine and scrape the bottom of the pan with a wooden spoon. Add tomatoes, paste, salt and pepper. Bring to a simmer and cook for about an hour, stirring occasionally. Taste and adjust salt and pepper to your personal preference.

Mussels Fra Diavolo

3 tbsp. canola oil

2 tbsp. unsalted butter

1 tsp. red pepper flakes

2 cloves garlic; minced

2 lbs. mussels; cleaned

1 cup of white wine

2 cups red sauce

¼ cup parsley

In a large, heavy sauté pan, heat oil and butter. Add the pepper flakes and garlic and stir. Making sure the pan is very hot, add mussels and white wine. Next, stir in the red sauce. Cover pan and cook until mussels open; about 2 minutes. Remove cover and toss the mussels in the sauce until each mussel is well coated. Add parsley and stir again. Transfer to serving dish and serve. Accompany with crunchy sauce to mop up all the delicious sauce.

Beef Tenderloin with Chimmichurri

Chimmichurri Sauce

1 bunch fresh, flat leaf parsley

1 bunch fresh cilantro

3 cloves garlic; minced

1 tsp. red pepper flakes

1 cup canola oil

1 cup olive oil

¼ cup red wine vinegar

½ tsp. sea salt

Chop parsley, cilantro and garlic in a food processor until finely
cut. Transfer to a ceramic or glass bowl. Stir in pepper flakes,

oils, vinegar & salt. You can use this right away, but it tastes much better if sits for a day or two.

1 2lb. piece of beef tenderloin

Sea salt and freshly cracked black pepper

1 tbsp. canola oil

Preheat oven to 350°.

Generously season all sides of the beef tenderloin with salt and pepper. Heat oil in a large, heavy skillet. Brown tenderloin on all sides. Transfer to oven and roast; 30 minutes for medium rare or 45 minutes for medium. Transfer to serving platter and let the meat "rest" for 10 minutes. Slice and serve with a little or a lot of the yummy chimmichurri sauce.

Depending where you live, fava beans go by many different names. Here, in North America, we call this vegetable a fava bean, derived from the Italian word "fava" which literally means bean. In the UK they are sold under the names broad beans or Windsor beans. Some varieties of this plant produce smaller, harder beans, which are sold under the monikers of horse bean, field beans or tic beans.

Fava Bean and Pea Salad With Lardons

1 lb. slab bacon; cut in ½" strips

2 cups fava beans; cooked

1 cup summer peas; cooked

6 cherry tomatoes; halved

½ small red onion; cut in thick slices

1 cup olive oil

1/3 cup red wine vinegar

½ tsp. Dijon mustard

Salt & pepper to taste

Heat a heavy skillet until very hot, add bacon. Reduce heat to medium and cook until both sides are crispy. Place bacon on a paper towel to cool.

In a large salad bowl, mix together beans, peas, tomatoes & onions. In a small bowl whisk together oil, vinegar, mustard, salt & pepper. Pour dressing over salad and toss.

Remove fat from bacon and place bacon "lardons" on top of salad. Enjoy.

Lavender Panna Cotta

1 ½ tsp. powdered gelatin

2 tablespoons cold water

1 cup 18% cream;

1/4 cup wildflower honey

1 vanilla bean; cut in half lengthwise and seeds scraped out

1 teaspoon food grade dried lavender

1 cup milk

1 drop each red and blue food coloring (this is optional)

In a small bowl sprinkle the gelatin over the 2 tablespoons of water and let soften for at least 5 minutes. Lightly grease 4 5-ounce ramekins with non stick baking spray.   Set aside.

In a small sauce pan, heat the cream, honey, vanilla bean and seeds& dried lavender. Bring to a gentle simmer then turn off the heat. Let stand for 10 minutes. Whisk again and then strain into a mixing bowl. Whisk in the gelatin for at least a minute to make sure it is very evenly distributed and that there are no lumps. Whisk in the milk and food coloring. Remember, the food coloring is optional.

Pour evenly into the ramekins and refrigerate for at least 6 hours or overnight. When you are ready to serve, gently run a butter knife around the rim of the ramekin and invert panna cotta to a serving plate. Garnish with a fresh sprig of lavender or use can use fresh berries or whipping cream.

★ CANCER ★
JUNE 22 - JULY 23
★ THE NURTURER ★

ELEMENT: WATER
RULING PLANET: MOON
GEMSTONE: PEARL

PERSONAL PROFILE -- CANCER FEMALE

Cancer is a water sign. This female is totally capable of circumventing every imaginable emotion and mood in a very short period of time. She is a moonchild, and her feelings are constantly being pulled in every direction. She is warm and loving and makes a wonderful mother, sister, friend and wife. This subject makes a poor mistress; she is after a permanent, stable relationship with home and children.

The Cancer female, unlike the talkative Gemini, is not a gossip. If there is a secret you feel you must share, it is safe with this lunar female. She will listen sympathetically and honor your words with secrecy. Her dedication and loyalty are true…she will always be there when you need her.

Cancer females have an outstanding memory, and years later she can recall conversations and probably what the person was wearing. This makes her a natural history buff, and this subject can encompass much of spare time. She may also take up genealogy, so she can trace her family tree.

All Cancers are collectors of something or other, and the female tends to concentrate on antiques to elaborate her consummate interest in days gone by. These may adorn her home along with pictures of her family members.

She loves her home, and will spend much time decorating it in a somewhat old-fashioned manner. You will be sure to find an assortment or collection of old recipe cards handed down over the generations. Grandma's hand written recipe cards would be well honored in this lady's kitchen. Her kitchen will be the focal point of her home; it will be warm and inviting, as she spends so much of her time there providing sustenance for her beloved family. This factor makes the Cancer woman a superb cook. You can trust that her need for security will keep her refrigerator, freezer, and cupboards bulging with provisions. She thinks that one can never have too much food, just in case. Even when her husband brings the boys home for dinner, unannounced, or a friend just stops by, she can still manage to whip up a gourmet meal that is bound to impress.

The lunar woman believes in quality. This is reflected in her wardrobe as well as the other areas in her life. She wants what she buys to last, so she tends to purchase fabrics and jewelry that add to her air of style and charm. This lady is a class act all the way!

PERSONAL PROFILE -- CANCER MALE

The Cancer male is not an open book; he keeps things "close to his vest". This doesn't mean he's overly secretive, it just means that he feels deeply and doesn't always display his emotions for fear of being hurt. Once a Cancer man opens his heart, he loves wholeheartedly and with all of his being.

Women will enjoy his company, because the Cancer man is the epitome of gallantry -- being courteous and protective of the female sex. Unlike some males, the lunar man is also a very good listener. He can be deeply compassionate, and is eager to help a friend out with a problem. His sharp flair for analysis can cut through the weightiest of dilemmas. You can always count on this man when you need him.

The Cancer male can make a very eloquent speaker. Like the female, he will amaze with his fantastic memory and total recall. This makes him an excellent historian, genealogist or professional speaker. He will always do his research and deliver an informative and accurate presentation.

He enjoys good food and drink. This man will have a special place in his heart for his mother's or grandmother's cooking. You could hear this man reminiscing about a favorite dish that he had as a child. If you really want to do something special for this guy, find out what his favorite childhood dish is and replicate it. No, it won't be the same as Mom's, but he will be touched that you went through the effort to make it for him…and he won't forget it!

This man is sensitive and very sentimental. He likes to hold on to old friends forever, and someone who was once in his heart will never be forgotten. He probably still keeps in touch with his boyhood friends.

This is a man who defers to his home and family. He prefers to entertain in his own domain, rather than spend time in unfamiliar surroundings. He enjoys puttering around in his back yard, garden, and workshop. He can be quite the handy man. This gentleman's home is truly his sanctuary.

This male may watch his dollars carefully, but he is not cheap. He would rather buy a top quality item instead of a cheap replica. He wants what he buys to last.

This is a very complex man, not easy to understand, but not dull either. Unlike some, he makes a very loyal friend or mate.

FAMOUS CANCERS

Lionel Messi	Selena Gomez
Tom Cruise	Luke Bryan
Tom Hanks	Alex Trebek
Liv Tyler	Sophia Vergara
Robin Williams	Ariana Grande
Sylvester Stallone	Khloe Kardashian

HERBS AND FOODS ASSOCIATED WITH CANCER

White Cabbage	Red Cabbage
Turnips	Shellfish
Dairy Products	Strawberries
Lemon	Tarragon

FLOWERS AND PLANTS

Maple Leaf	Verbena
Lily	Acanthus
White Rose	Convolvulus
Geranium	

AROMATHERAPY

Chamomile, Lemon Verbena, Rose Water, Strawberry

SET THE TABLE AND BRING THE WINE

General advice when inviting a Cancer male or female to your home: never take anything for granted. If he shows up in a new suit, comment on it. If she is sporting a new hairstyle, tell her how lovely she looks. Remember how sensitive they are. Make it clear in your flatteries that you are being sincere.

Melodic music, softly played in the background will put the Cancer silently in tune with the celestial harmonies. It will bring out their best moods, ensuring that they will be congenial dinner guests.

Cancer is one of the more traditional signs, so a formal table setting is appropriate here. Since Cancer is a water sign, they find water soothing. In the warm weather, dinner by the pool would be conducive to a serene evening. If you are geographically fortunate enough to live on the coast, take your *moonchild* for a picnic on the beach.

Cancers love food and can be seduced by the scintillating aromas of a slow cooked dish. It would be clever of you to appeal to the Cancer person to help you in the kitchen. Both genders are excellent cooks and feel more than comfortable hovering over the stove. Also, you could ask the Cancer male when giving the invitation, what his Mom's favorite recipes are, so you can include them in your menu plan. Cancer men revere their mothers, and often spend and always have time for them. He is a good son.

Whatever you serve as a main course, include lemon meringue pie or lemon square as the dessert! I have **never** met a Cancer who doesn't list it as a favorite, if not **the** favorite dessert of all times. Strawberry is also a popular flavor.

If you take the time to create the proper mood for these lunar children, your reward will be a successful and enjoyable evening.

Here are some menu plans that should produce strong **Mood Magic**.

If you are not geographically located in a place where fresh oysters are readily available, try your local supermarket. Most high end grocery stores sell fresh oysters in the seafood section.

Oysters With Bacon & Spinach

12 ceramic oyster shells (for baking and serving)

2 tablespoons butter

1 tablespoon all purpose flour

1 cup whipping cream

Dash of nutmeg

8 ounces meaty bacon; chopped

4 cups baby spinach: cleaned & stemmed

1 clove garlic: minced

1/8 teaspoon cayenne pepper

2 tablespoons dry white wine

1 tsp. brandy or cognac

2 tablespoons grated Pecorino Romano cheese

12 medium oysters

1 cup fresh breadcrumbs

2 lemons; cut in wedges

Melt butter in small skillet over medium heat. Add flour; whisk 2 minutes. Add cream slowly and whisk until mixture thickens slightly. Stir in nutmeg and remove from heat.

Sauté bacon in heavy large skillet over medium heat until crisp, about 6 minutes. Transfer bacon to paper towels to drain. Discard all but 2 tablespoons drippings from skillet. Add spinach, garlic, nutmeg and cayenne to skillet and sauté over medium heat until vegetables are soft, about 2 minutes. Add wine and cook until absorbed, about 15 seconds. Add cream mixture and bring to simmer. Stir until spinach mixture thickens slightly, about 3 minutes. Stir in bacon, brandy and cheese. Season generously with salt and pepper. Remove from heat.

Preheat oven to 500°F.

Place 1 oyster on a ceramic shell. Top each oyster with about 2 tablespoons spinach mixture... Place on rimmed baking sheet. (Can be made 4 hours ahead. Cover and chill.)

Top each oyster with breadcrumbs. Bake until spinach mixture
bubbles and crumbs are golden, about 8 minutes.
Serve with lemon wedges.

Pan Seared Filet Mignon w/ Herb Butter

2 tbsp. butter

2 4-6 oz filet mignon steaks

2 tbsp. butter

Pinch of dried thyme

Pinch of paprika

1 tsp. parsley; minced

salt & pepper to taste

Heat a skillet to medium-high heat. Season both sides of steaks with salt & pepper. Cook until desired doneness; about 3 minutes per side for medium rare. While steaks are cooking, combine remaining ingredients. Form two balls of butter. Transfer steaks to plate and place one butter ball atop each steak. Delicious!

The Po'Boy Sandwich was invented in New Orleans in the 1930's and is traditionally filled with oysters, shrimp or catfish. This next recipe is a delicious variation of this southern classic. It is filled with fried chicken breast and tangy coleslaw, but you can substitute shrimp or white fish if you like. No matter how you make it, it is simply delicious!

Fried Chicken Po'Boy

2 cups shredded white cabbage

2 cups shredded red cabbage

1 small red onion; thinly sliced

2 cups good quality mayonnaise

1 tbsp. fresh lemon juice

Dash hot sauce

½ tsp. celery seeds

Salt and pepper to taste

2 large chicken breast; butterflied & pounded thin

1 cup all purpose flour

1 tsp. cayenne pepper

½ tsp. salt

½ tsp. garlic powder

½ cup canola oil

Good quality buns

2 tbsp. butter

In a large bowl, combine the cabbage and onion and mix well. In another mixing bowl, whisk together mayonnaise, lemon juice, hot sauce, celery seeds, salt and pepper. Pour dressing over cabbage blend and toss until all the cabbage and onion is coated. Set aside.

Combine flour, cayenne, salt & garlic powder together in a shallow bowl. Dredge flattened chicken in flour and shake off the excess. Heat oil in a heavy skillet on medium high heat. Add chicken breast and cook until golden brown and cooked through; about 4 minutes each side. If your chicken starts to get to brown, reduce the heat a little. These should be golden brown. Remove chicken and place on paper towels.

Butter each side of the buns and brown, face down in a clean frying pan. You want the bun to be golden brown on the bottom, yet still soft.

Spoon some slaw on the bottom of the bun and top with fried chicken and top with the bun top.

Lemon Cheesecake with Strawberry Topping

For crust

1/3 cup whole almonds

2/3 cup graham cracker crumbs

1/4 cup sugar

1/4 cup (1/2 stick) unsalted butter, melted

Finely grind almonds in a food processor. Add graham cracker crumbs, sugar and butter. Process until clumps form. Press mixture onto bottom (not sides) of 9-inch-diameter spring form pan with 2 3/4-inch-high sides. Chill 30 minutes.

For cheesecake

2 8oz. packages cream cheese

2 eggs

1/2 cups sugar, divided

1tsp. vanilla

1 tbsp. fresh lemon juice

½ tsp. lemon zest

Preheat oven to 325°F. Cream the cheese (easy to do if it's at room temperature). Add eggs, one at a time, and then beat in sugar, vanilla, lemon juice and zest. Pour over crust. Bake for 40 minutes. Let cool, then cover, and refrigerate until ready to serve. Serve topped with strawberry sauce.

Strawberry Sauce

2 cups fresh strawberries; hulled, cleaned & sliced in half

½ cup of powdered sugar

¼ cup of Amaretto Liqueur

Mix all ingredients together. Cover and let rest at 30 minutes before serving. Can be made a day ahead and refrigerated.

LEO

JULY 23 - AUGUST 22
★ THE ENTERTAINER ★

ELEMENT: FIRE
RULING PLANET: SUN
GEMSTONE: RUBY / PERIDOT

PERSONAL PROFILE -- LEO FEMALE

This fire sign female has many noteworthy attributes. Chances are if you don't notice them yourself, she will be happy to apprise you of them. She totally understands that Leo is the King, or in this case, Queen of the jungle. She will flaunt her regal heir proudly. Some people may perceive her attitude as snobby; she prefers to think of it as just being appropriately selective. This disposition extends itself to the company she keeps and just about every other aspect of her life.

You can't fail but to be attracted to her; she is almost always the center of attention. She thrives on, and demands this very focal point. Don't ever question her loyalty; it is strong and true.

At their best, Leo females are affectionate, enthusiastic, cheerful, optimistic people. She indeed feels that her mission in life is to bring sunshine into other people's lives. It is a much-needed quality that this woman should not neglect. Caring and sharing are natural to her; it is **her mission** to realize that others must sometimes come first.

This lady will dress splendidly, having impeccable hair, make-up, and jewelry. Rubies are her favorite gem, but the gold earrings, necklaces, and thick bracelets will also be strongly accented. This flair for decoration will also manifest itself in the Leo's home. No matter what her financial status, this woman will manage to create a lair of some magnificence for those lucky enough to be invited into her domain. You may find an overstuffed sofa adorned with jewel colored throw pillows and a rich tapestry hanging on the wall. Her style will be opulent. She makes a marvelous hostess, as seeing to her guests' comforts will be her principle priority. She must feel that she has made a favorable impression, and go to great lengths to accomplish this objective, even if it's not in the budget.

PERSONAL PROFILE -- LEO MALE

This man is highly organized and creative. He exudes self confidence, optimism and charm. Have a problem that needs a solution? Just ask him. The Leo male will be happy to listen and then more than willing to lend a helping hand. He needs to feel that what he does matters and is appreciated. So if your Leo does help you out, AND HE WILL, don't skimp on the thanks and praise. Scratch this cat and hear him purr.

He will display expansive, optimistic, and self-confident attributes. There should be an abundance of energy, although the typical lion often forgets that the body can wear out. He pushes it to the point of exhaustion, whether in the pursuit of pleasure or vocational success. Expect generosity and benevolence, but also comprehend that this man will wait for admiration and appreciation in return.

This man treats his home as his castle, and his love of luxury will be evident throughout. You might expect his sofa to be nine feet long and covered in crush velvet. The Leo man is a sun worshiper and it is an innate feeling that he needs light to flourish. He will collect lamps in the same fashion as some collect sculpture or paintings and mirrors will be everywhere, even in the oddest places. This is because the Leo is fascinated with his own image. You might even find a looking glass in such an unlikely place as his linen closet.

This man's strong love of beauty is also seen in his choice of female companions. His ego demands that he sports a pretty girl on his arm.

This pussycat is playful and fun loving.

You may think that this demanding, attention-loving man might prove to be insufferable, but the truth is that when looking at the big picture, his incessant love of life leads him to be a worthy companion.

FAMOUS LEOS

Jennifer Lawrence	Madonna
Jennifer Lopez	Charlize Theron
Sean Penn	Barack Obama
Amy Adams	Arnold Schwarzenegger
Demi Lovato	Helen Mirren

HERBS AND FOODS ASSOCIATED WITH LEO

Bay Leaves	Honeycomb
Spinach	Cereals
Walnuts	Olives
Saffron	Peppermint
Rosemary	Veal
Rice	Watercress
Beets	

FLOWERS AND PLANTS

Sunflower
Marigold
Celandine

Passionflower
Olive Tree
Citrus Trees

AROMATHERAPY

Peppermint, Rose Petal, Rosemary

SET THE TABLE AND BRING THE WINE

Leo's have a distinctive flair for drama, and at your party, these people are more than likely to make themselves the center of attention. They will be sure to entertain your other guests. They are outgoing and bubbly, and will regale your company with stories of their many escapades.

Leo's feel they have a right to the best of everything, so it would be wise to decorate your home splendidly for the occasion. Since they are ruled by the sun, adorn your table with all shades of yellow, orange and gold. A bouquet of sunflowers would be the perfect flower arrangement. Organizing outings come naturally to the lion and lioness, so feel free to ask for their suggestions regarding decor and menu planning. They would be delighted to assist you with these details, as it is a compliment to their always-hungry egos. Prestige and presentation are paramount to this guest, so whatever preparations you implement, go all out for flamboyance. It will be noticed and appreciated, because Leo has a strong tendency to barrage a person with effusive, but sincere accolades. They literally gush. Being generous people, the host will likely be presented with a bottle of wine or other hostess gift. Make sure you complement them on how much you like it. They like to know that their benevolence is appreciated.

Leo's love people, so give your event the vibe of being a party. Loud music with room to dance up a storm would go over very well. A costume party, or Murder Mystery Dinner where the Leo could really ham it up, both would be a winner. If it is more of a business setting, turn it into a fashionable cocktail party. Whichever format you choose, make the Leo feel like the guest of honor. Steer the conversation around to them and their achievements. That kind of attention will make the Leo a satisfied and contented recipient of you very special efforts. Last word. Make sure your food and beverage list is of the same caliber of opulence as your ambience.

Congratulations on a job well done!

Here are some menu plans that are sure to please your Leo guest.

When we think of caviar, we automatically think of it as something only the wealthy can afford to eat. Truth be told, there are several affordable types of caviar. There are many types of American caviar varieties to choose from that don't cost a fortune. Your Leo guest will be totally impressed!

Caviar with Toast Points

8 pieces of sliced baguette or country bread

Olive oil for brushing

½ cup crème fraiche

1 small tin of caviar

Chives for garnish

Preheat oven to 350°. Brush a little olive oil on bread and bake until crisp; about 12 minutes. Remove from oven and let cool. Arrange toast points on a platter. Top each toast with a dollop of crème fraiche and top with a small spoonful of caviar. Garnish with a sliver of chive. That's it; this decadent appetizer couldn't be any simpler.

If you don't have the time to make aioli, don't worry. You can "cheat" by mixing 1 cup of good quality store bought mayonnaise, 1 tbsp. of fresh lemon juice and 1 small clove of minced garlic. Garnish with a wedge of lemon and voilla!! Only you have to know.

Cracked, Cold Lobster W/ Lemon Aioli

1 -1 lb lobster: cooked, cleaned and chilled

(You can buy an already cooked and cleaned lobster in your local seafood market or supermarket)

Aioli

1 clove garlic; minced

Pinch of sea salt

1 egg yolk

¼ tsp. Dijon mustard

¾ cup extra virgin olive oil

1 tsp. fresh lemon juice

Cracked, black pepper to taste

In a small metal bowl mix together minced garlic, salt, egg yolk and mustard. Slowly add olive oil, whisking constantly until mixture emulsifies. Whisk in lemon juice and pepper. Chill for at least 1 hour before serving.

On a pretty plate, place a fancy, shallow glass in the center (like a martini glass). Spoon aioli in center of glass. Arrange lobster meat around the base of the glass. Garnish with fresh chives and lemon wedges.

If you don't have a paella pan, don't fret, a good quality cast iron pan works very well with this dish.

Seafood Paella

1/2 cup olive oil

3 garlic cloves; minced

½ tsp. red pepper flakes

1 small onion; minced

1 roma tomato; diced fine

2 cups bomba rice (any short grain rice will do)

5 cups chicken stock; hot

Large pinch of saffron

¼ cup frozen peas

1 fillet firm, white fish, such as cod

12 mussels; cleaned

6 jumbo shrimp; cleaned and deveined.

Preheat oven to 375°.

In your cast iron skillet or paella pan, heat oil until hot, but not smoking. Add garlic, pepper flakes & onion. Sauté on medium until the onion wilts; about 5 minutes. Add tomato and stir. Add rice and stir until rice is well coated with oil and vegetable mixture. Start adding chicken stock 1 ladle at a time, constantly stirring so that the rice cooks evenly. When all the stock has been added, it should be cooked until wet, but not swimming in stock. If it looks too wet, continue to cook on the stovetop until the right consistency. Stir in the saffron and peas. Arrange the seafood in the pan pushing down on it, so it is "nestled" into the rice. Cook for an additional 3 minutes on the stovetop. Transfer to oven and continue to cook for 10 minutes. When you remove the dish from the oven, the mussels should all be open (discard any that do not open) and the shrimp a bright pink. Garnish with fresh parsley and serve.

This steak can be made on an outdoor grill, but since most people will be cooking in their homes, I have adapted it to the stovetop. If you do decide to make this on the grill, please use a charcoal grill instead of gas. It gives such a better flavor.

Tomahawk Steak with Rosemary Butter

1 2 1/2 pound tomahawk steak

Sea salt and pepper

4 tbsp. unsalted butter

1 sprig fresh rosemary minced

Preheat oven to 400°

Generously season steak with salt and pepper. Let stand on counter until room temperature. In a small bowl, combine butter and rosemary.

Heat a large heavy skillet, preferably cast iron until very hot. Add oil. Place steak in pan and sear without moving; about 5 minutes. Turn steak over and cook another 4 minutes. Transfer steak to a baking sheet and cook in oven another 12 minutes for medium rare and about 18 minutes for medium. Please do not overcook. Take out of oven and transfer to a wooden platter. Spread rosemary butter on top and let the steak rest for about 5 minutes. Slice and serve. Garnish with fresh rosemary.

★ VIRGO ★
AUGUST 23 - SEPTEMBER 22
★ THE HERBALIST ★

ELEMENT: EARTH

RULING PLANE: MERCURY

GEMSTONE: SARDONYX/SAPPHIRE

PERSONALITY PROFILE -- VIRGO FEMALE

The Virgo woman is an earth sign known for her sense of self-discipline and control. These females are extremely neat and well organized, believing that everything has a place. She takes great pride in her appearance and is always well groomed. This woman keeps her emotions under a tighter rein than most signs, and her innermost desires tend to remain her own secrets. She exudes an air of dignity and seriousness. She has mastered impeccable manners, and feels that one must always act like a lady.

A strong interest in self-improvement and hard work will keep this woman on a life-long journey of bettering herself. She handles details very well, which lead her to complete a very thorough job, whether it be cleaning her house or writing a brief.

The Virgo woman displays attributes of patience, kindness, and generosity, but her iron will manifest tremendous determination. Once a course is charted, she will remain firm and steadfast. She will utilize her considerable energies achieving her objectives, though she will be cautious in her progress, rather than headstrong. In her mind, this venue should ward off failure -- one of her worst fears.

Her home is her domain, and she will not shy away from housework in order to keep the premises squeaky clean. You will not see a littered kitchen counter top or a living room floor strewn with children's toys. Her system will keep everything in its place.

Her appearance tends to be as neat and tidy as her home, preferring practical clothing rather than the Leo's flamboyant style.

Being one of the most youthful of signs, this feminine figure will keep her good looks well into middle age and beyond. Think of Rachel Welch and Sophia Loren.

PERSONALITY PROFILE -- VIRGO MALE

The Virgo male is a master of mental work, and has a keen, methodical intellect. He is interested in almost anything that would further his personal career, and employs much of his leisure time in the pursuit of self-betterment. This man will be careful to watch what he eats and will take an active approach to a healthy lifestyle.

One of his strong suits is that in perusing a new prospect, his analytical mind can usually uncover any hidden risks involved. When he says no to a venture don't ask him twice. No means no. He uses this sense of discrimination in choosing his friends and business associates and rarely makes mistakes.

This man requires peaceful surroundings and lifestyle in order to function to his fullest. He does not like confrontation or acrimonious situations. If he does have any stressful situations in his life, he often works through it with exercise. He believes in taking care of himself and it shows through his diet and lifestyle. The man ordering the veggie burger across the restaurant room is probably a Virgo.

Many Virgo males remain bachelors well into adulthood. These men tend to hide in their work and leisure activities; guarding their emotions and feelings with great care. Once this Virgo male has decided to love, however, he will be a respectful and caring partner, sure never to miss an anniversary or birthday.

When it comes to career, they are systematic, cautious, and have a strong sense of honor and responsibility. Their introvert tendencies often keep them in the background. Rather than being the political candidate, they will be the campaign manager. In a large corporation, rather than being the CEO, they will be the comptroller or personal assistant. His love of detail makes him proficient at his work.

He doesn't wear *faddish* clothing. He prefers the conventional, semi-formal look. If you can convince him to wear blue jeans, he will insist on having them pressed. You will never find this man with greasy hair or a scraggly beard. He is as meticulous in his appearance as he is in his diction. Dry cleaners love him!

Like the Virgoan female, and because they are often bachelors, these men make excellent housekeepers. To live in a messy home would leave him feeling out of control in his whole life. He is also quite capable in the kitchen. This is because he knows what tastes and textures he prefers, so his attitude is that if you want something done right, do it yourself.

FAMOUS VIRGOS

Beyonce

Adam Sandler

Jimmy Fallon

Niall Horan

Warren Buffet

Jennifer Hudson

Mother Teresa

Blake Lively

Pink

Prince Harry

Colin Firth

Jada Pinkett Smith

Shania Twain

Agatha Christie

HERBS AND FOODS ASSOCIATED WITH VIRGO

Cardamom

Carrots

Purple Potatoes

Hazelnuts

Peanuts

Celeriac

Parsnips

Fiber

Kohlrabi

Almond

FLOWERS AND PLANTS

Acorn

Yellow Archangel

Forget-me-not

Nasturtium

Oak Leaf

Buttercup

Crosswort

Cat's Ear

AROMATHERAPY

Frankincense, cardamom

SET THE TABLE AND BRING THE WINE

When entertaining the Virgo, keep these things in mind. Socially, they like small parties immaculately catered or at least prepared. Sloppy eaters or careless smokers will be their least favorite co-diners. They love detail; so the cutting and design of the food will be of great importance; try to make a real effort to stylize your offerings. Don't be intimidated by this – just follow the recipes and do your best to present the dishes in a uniform fashion. It is also important to make sure to wash your hands before handling any food...Yes, this may sound simplistic, but Virgos will appreciate a very clean and organized kitchen and host! I would also recommend giving your house or apartment a good dusting before entertaining your Virgoan guest. One last thing, make sure there is plenty of antibacterial soap in the bathroom and clean hand towels... even better, paper towels.

Virgos are totally into health, so keep in mind that everything you prepare should be of the utmost freshness and highest level of nutrition. Fresh herbs should be used whenever possible, as with edible flowers. Since many Virgos are vegetarians, it is best to keep red meat to a minimum. You would be better off sticking with fish, poultry, and vegetable dishes. Virgos love to come into a home and smell the aroma of food cooking. Having said that, refrain from any potpourri, air fresheners or perfume. They will prefer to smell the food or fresh herbs. This can include a soup gently simmering on the stove or a casserole cooking in the oven. Since liquor does not coincide with good health, it is advisable to offer herbal teas and bottled water along with any wine or spirits. If you are serving beer, offer an organic lager.

Adorn the table with small flowers such as forget- me -nots and buttercups in small vases or cups...no oversized flower arrangement here. Keep the place setting simple and pretty as well. As I mentioned earlier, they are fond of small, intricate patterns, so keep this in mind when setting the table. For Virgo, simple elegance is the key. As for music, keep it low and in the background.

For entertainment, Virgos love intellectual parlor games. This can include Pictionary, Scrabble, and Trivial Pursuit. With their zest for detail, don't be surprised if they are the runaway winners.

The Virgoan dinner party will be on a quieter scale than those for more outgoing signs. But the innate intelligence and grace of this sign will certainly provide for an entertaining evening.

Here are some healthy suggestions for your next Virgoan dinner party.

Carrot & Butternut Squash Soup

2 tbsp. canola oil

2 tbsp. butter

3 carrots; peeled and chopped

1 large potato; peeled and chopped

1 butternut squash; peeled and chopped

1 small onion; diced

1 tsp. fresh ginger; minced

½ tsp. sea salt

½ tsp. cracked black pepper

4 cups vegetable stock; warm

¼ cup crème fraiche or sour cream

Pumpkin seeds for garnish (optional)

In a large heavy stock pot, heat oil and butter to medium high heat. Add carrots, potato, squash & onion. Sauté until vegetable begin to soften; about 6 minutes. Add ginger, salt and pepper and stir well. Add vegetable stock and bring to a simmer. Cook until vegetable and tender; about 15 minutes. Remove from heat. Gently puree soup with a hand blender. Be careful, the soup is hot. When the soup is a smooth consistency, return to heat and gently warm up; do not boil. Right before you serve the soup, remove from heat and stir in the sour cream or crème fraiche. Serve immediately. Garnish with pumpkin seeds (optional).

The Astrological Kitchen by Angela Buck

Penne W/ Shrimp, Roasted Tomatoes & Pesto

1 cup fresh parsley

½ cup fresh basil leaves

1 tbsp. pine nuts

½ cup olive oil

2 garlic cloves

Pinch of salt

12 cherry tomatoes; cut in half

12 large shrimp; cleaned and deveined

¼ cup olive oil

½ tsp. sea salt

1/4tsp. black pepper

1 package of dried penne

Pinch red pepper flakes

¼ cup white wine

½ cup grated parmesan cheese

Preheat oven to 350°

To make the pesto, blend first 6 ingredients in a food processor. Set aside. Toss tomatoes, shrimp, olive oil, salt and pepper in a bowl until well coated. Transfer to baking dish and bake until shrimp are cooked and tomatoes are beginning to wilt; about 12 minutes. Cook penne until al dente. Meanwhile, heat pesto in a large sauté pan. Add pepper flakes, shrimp and cherry tomatoes (make sure to add all the juices and olive oil from sheet pan to the pot). Add wine and bring to a simmer.

Add pasta and toss until well coated. Add cheese and toss to coat. Transfer to serving dish and serve immediately.

Farro & Root Vegetable Stuffed Squash

1 cup uncooked farro; rinsed

1 small red onion; finely diced

1 parsnip; peeled and diced

1carrot; peeled and diced

¼ cup hazelnuts

2 tbsp. olive oil

Salt & pepper to taste

1 squash; butternut or acorn

1 tbsp. butter

Pinch of salt

Preheat oven to 350°

In a small saucepan, cover farro with cold water and bring to a boil. Reduce heat and simmer until tender; about 30 minutes. Drain and set aside. Toss onion, parsnip, carrot, hazelnuts, olive oil and salt and pepper to coat. Transfer mixture to a sheet pan and roast until tender; about 20 minutes. Remove from oven and add vegetable mixture to the faro. Cut squash in half lengthwise. Scoop out seeds. Rub squash with butter and season with salt. Cover with foil. Put on same sheet pan and bake until tender; about 30 minutes. Remove foil, being careful not to burn yourself on the steam. Fill squash with the faro mixture and put back in the oven until brown; about 10 minutes. Serve immediately.

Roasted Vegetable & Chicken Bake

2 chicken breasts; season with salt & pepper

2 large white potatoes; cut in quarters

2 purple potatoes; cut in quarters

1 large red onion; cut in quarters

2 large carrots; peeled and chopped

¼ cup olive oil

2 tsp. fresh thyme; minced

2 tsp. fresh rosemary

1 tsp. sea salt

1 tsp. garlic powder

Black pepper to taste

1 cup chicken stock

Preheat oven to 350°

Toss potatoes, onion, carrots, oil, fresh herbs, garlic powder, salt & pepper until well coated. Transfer to a large baking dish. Pour chicken stock over vegetables. Place chicken breasts on top of the vegetables, pressing down slightly. Bake for 40 minutes. Let cool slightly before serving.

Avocado Popsicles

2 large, ripe avocados; pitted

1 14 oz. sweetened condensed milk

1 tbsp. fresh lime juice

½ tsp. lime zest

2 cups heavy cream

1 tbsp. honey

In a food processor, blend avocado flesh, condensed milk, lime juice and zest. Pulse until smooth. Beat heavy cream and honey until stiff peak form. Fold heavy cream into avocado. Put into popsicle molds and freeze at least 4 hours, Enjoy.

★ LIBRA ★
SEPTEMBER 23 - OCTOBER 22
★ THE HARMONIZER ★

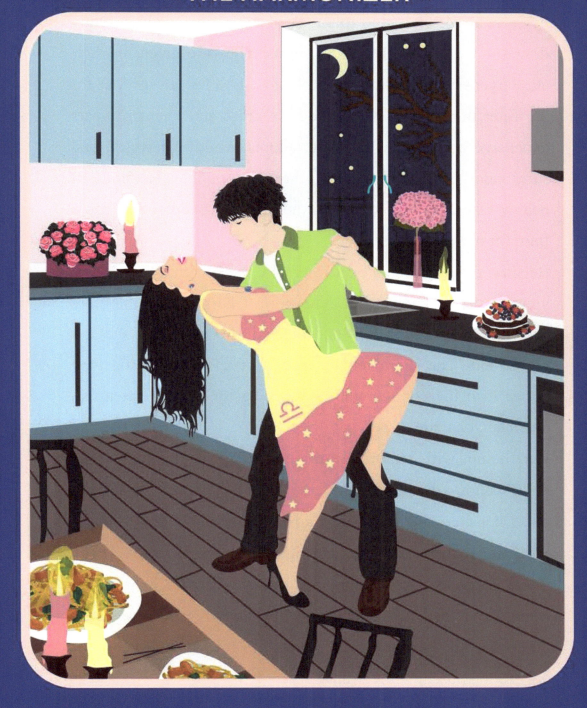

ELEMENT: AIR
RULING PLANET: VENUS
GEMSTONE: TOURMALINE / OPAL

PERSONAL PROFILE -- LIBRA FEMALE

Libra is an air sign, and this makes the Libra female strongly drawn to esthetic beauty in all forms. They are noted for their attractiveness and delicate complexion. She has an instinct for the finer things. She is fastidious in dress and manner, wears expensive and sensual perfume, adores beautiful jewelry, and surrounds herself with luxury wherever possible. Her love of beauty extends itself to music, the arts and people. She has a flare for elegance.

Because this is the sign of partnership, the Libran lady tends to view her companion as an extension of herself, and therefore demands the same level of excellence in her mate that she sets for herself. The Libra female tends to prefer the artistic type rather than the commercial. She can easily fall for the artist, musician, or writer type.

Her home will be artistically decorated with pastels, the coordination of colors being evident throughout. Once she picks her color pattern, such as rose gold, this hue will show itself in her rugs, furniture, and right down to the linens. If she is not happy in her surroundings, she will not be happy with herself, as it makes her feel out of balance. Fresh flowers will more than likely, always be present, as they are pleasing not only to the nose, but the eye.

This woman is basically a person of even temper and is usually able to find the silver lining in every cloud. If she is displaying any sense of stubbornness or strong will, soft persuasion will be the only way to break that mood.

Extremely feminine, she is also clever, articulate and fascinating. The Libra female is the epitome of charm.

PERSONAL PROFILE -- LIBRA MALE

Like the female, the Libra male is born under the sign of the scales, so balance and harmony will be his objectives. His sensitive nature is at its best when his immediate world is ruled by order and serenity.

The Libra is not your typical athletic type. Rather than watching or participating in sports, give him a tablet or board game such as chess or backgammon and his interest will peak.

The Libra has a strong sense of justice and will give everyone an even chance to prove him or herself. He is tactful and makes the perfect diplomat. Although he is by nature peaceable, he will strongly react to an obvious injustice; this makes this man a perfect arbitrator, lawyer and judge.

His appearance and his home must both illustrate that strong sense of harmony and balance that we have explained under the Libra female. These men lean toward the silky fabrics as opposed to the wools and tweeds. He will always look perfectly put together.

Even if he is not responsible for the main decorating of his home, he will always offer artistic suggestions, and trust him to supply the finishing touches, such as tasteful pieces of art.

This is a charming, attractive man with an exaggerated sense of fair play and justice.

FAMOUS LIBRANS

Kate Winslet	Kim Kardashian
Eminem	Vladimir Putin
Will Smith	Gwen Stefani
Gwyneth Paltrow	Marion Cotillard
James McCord	Matt Damon
Hugh Jackman	Sting

HERBS AND FOODS ASSOCIATED WITH LIBRA

Legumes	Maple Syrup
Barley	Cereals
Berries	Mint
Basil	Cayenne
Apple	Artichokes
Ginger	Lettuce
Pears	Grapes

FLOWERS AND PLANTS

Ash	Poplar
Daisy	Bluebell
Rose	Apple Trees
Hydrangea	Maple Tree

AROMATHERAPY

Apple blossom, geranium, rose, orange amber

SET THE TABLE AND BRING THE WINE

Libras are full of life and love to have a great time. They are a lot of fun to be with, and this makes them very popular dinner guests. To the host, in the very nicest ways, the Libra knows how to show appreciation. Since they are very social creatures, they prove to be very interactive and warm with the other guests. The last thing to expect from these guests is to have a picky eater or drinker.

Libras enjoy a balanced meal, meaning all four-food groups must be represented. They look to the color schemes of the food and decor. The textures they prefer are soft and crunchy. They prefer to have the opportunity to take the foods they feel will balance their meal. They enjoy an open seating format, this way they can choose their own seat for the company they feel is compatible for them. If it must be a sit down affair, again to balance the atmosphere, they prefer the seating to be male female, male female pattern. Also, take the time to place fresh flowers at the table...short cut roses or hydrangea would make the perfect centerpiece.

They love the balance of sweet and sour foods and an Asian variety is perfect to please their palette. The desserts should be very rich and creamy, such as ice cream with a caramel topping. They can then be totally contradictory and like a piece of melon with a dash of salt. Remember how they like to balance opposites.

The mood should be mellow and the background music soothing. It can even be a classical theme. Remember that board games can be used as an after dinner activity. You will find that this personality will be the life of the party, and they have the kind of charm and sense of humor that will make your soiree one to be talked about for months to come.

Here are some balanced meals sure to bring harmony to your Libran dinner party.

> **Tom Yam Kung is a very traditional Thai staple. Librans will love the spicy and creamy contrasts to this delicious soup. Kaffir lime leaves, lemongrass, galangal, Nam Prik Pao & Bird's Eye Chilies are readily available in any Asian market. Don't be intimidated by this soup, it is VERY easy to make.**

Tom Yam Kung

2 cups good quality chicken broth

6 fresh kaffir lime leaves, torn into pieces

8 slices of lemongrass

8 very thin slices of galangal

2 tbsp. Nam Prik Pao

4 fresh bird's eye chilies; crushed

1 lb. jumbo shrimp; cleaned and deveined (the head & tail are optional)

1 cup coconut milk

¼ cup fresh lime juice

¼ cup fish sauce

¼ cup fresh cilantro leaves

In a saucepan, bring stock to a gentle simmer, making sure not to boil. Add lime leaves, lemongrass and galangal. Simmer for about 15 minutes to infuse all the flavors. Stir in Nam Prik Pao, chilies and shrimp. Simmer until shrimp are firm; about 4 minutes. Stir in coconut milk and bring back to a gentle simmer. Remove from heat and stir in lime juice and fish sauce. Add cilantro and serve immediately. Note: leave the lemongrass, lime leaves and galangal in the bowl, but don't eat them. They are discarded when you are finished the soup.

Balsamic vinegar has been used in kitchens for centuries. It dates back to the middle ages as far back as 1046! It is made from grape must and aged in cherry or oak barrels. Librans will like the balance of the vinegar with the sweetness of the honey.

Honey Balsamic Pork Chops W/ Sautéed Apples

2 thick cut pork chops

Salt & pepper

2 tbsp. canola oil

1 medium granny smith apple; peeled and diced

2 tbsp. butter

Pinch of nutmeg

1 cup balsamic vinegar

½ cup liquid honey

Season chops with salt and pepper. In a small skillet, sauté apples in butter until they begin to get soft; about 3 minutes. Add nutmeg and stir. Remove from heat. In a small sauce pan, whisk together vinegar and honey and bring to a simmer. Stir this sauce frequently until it begins to thicken; about 3 minutes. Remove from heat. In a large, heavy skillet heat oil over medium high heat. Add pork chops and cook until both sides are a golden brown and chops are cooked through; about 4 – 5 minutes per side. When chops are almost done, spoon a little sauce over chops and cook about a minute longer or until sauce begins to bubble on chops.

Arrange pork chops on serving platter and spoon a little sauce over top. Next spoon a little apple mixture on top. This makes a perfect fall or winter dinner.

Chicken Stuffed With Pears W/Maple Glaze

2 large chicken breasts; butterflied and seasoned with salt & pepper

2 cups fresh pears; peeled and diced

¼ cup cooked quinoa

1/2 small red onion; minced

1 tsp. fresh thyme; minced

1 egg; beaten

1 tbsp. butter; melted

Salt & pepper

Preheat oven to 350°

Bring maple syrup, juice and zest to a boil. Simmer and reduce by half; the mixture should be syrupy. Set aside.

In a small bowl, mix together pears, quinoa, onion, thyme, egg, butter and salt & pepper. Stuff mixture into chicken breasts. Drizzle about half of the glaze over chicken breasts and bake until done; about 20 minutes. Remove from oven and spoon a little more of the glaze over top.

Chicken Gyoza w/ Garlic Dipping Sauce

1 tbsp. rice wine vinegar

2 tbsp. sugar

2 tbsp. soy sauce

2 tbsp. sherry

1 tsp. sriracha

1 garlic clove; minced

½ tsp. fresh ginger; minced

1 tbsp. cornstarch

2 tbsp. water

½ tsp. balsamic vinegar

Combine rice wine vinegar, sugar, soy sauce, sherry, sriracha, garlic, ginger. Heat mixture in a small saucepan until a mild simmer. Stir together cornstarch and water in a small bowl and whisk into pot. Continue whisking until sauce thickens. Remove from heat and stir in balsamic vinegar. Set aside.

½ pound ground, cooked chicken (you can use pork or shrimp)

½ tsp. red pepper flakes

1 tsp. fresh ginger; minced

1 garlic clove; minced

1 tsp. cornstarch

2 tsp. sherry

2 basil leaves; torn into small pieces

1 package wonton wrappers

3 tbsp. canola or peanut oil

3 tbsp. green onion; minced

Mix all ingredients (except won ton wrappers) in a small bowl until well incorporated. Put a small amount of filling in the middle of each wrapper. Dip your fingertips in a little water and "pinch" the ends of the wrappers to make a little purse.

The wrappers must be well sealed so that the filling doesn't fall out.

Heat oil over medium high heat. Gently add the wontons and brown on both sides. Serve with garlic dipping sauce on the side. Garnish with a little chopped chive or green onion.

★ SCORPIO ★

OCTOBER 23 - NOVEMBER 22
★ PASSIONATE ★

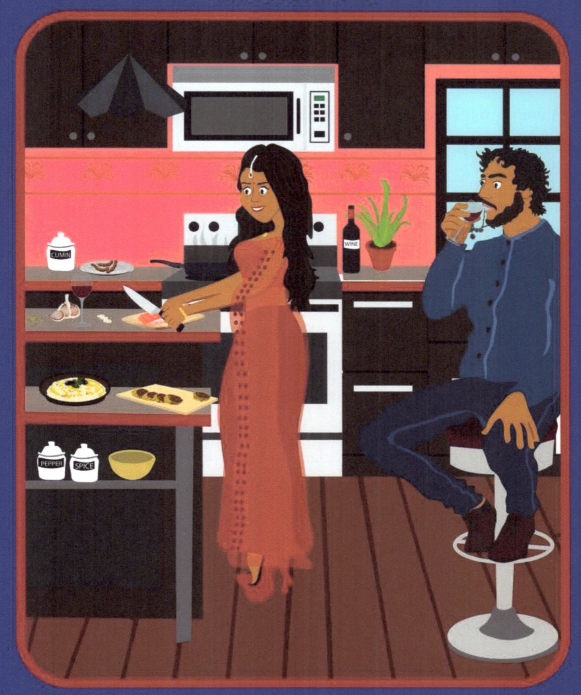

ELEMENT: WATER

RULING PLANET: PLUTO

GEMSTONE: TOPAZ

PERSONALITY PROFILE -- SCORPIO FEMALE

This is a water sign, making the Scorpio woman extremely intense and emotional. She is one of the most sensual of all the signs; having hypnotic eyes and a sensual, sultry voice.

The Scorpio woman takes life seriously; so don't try to fool her. Superficiality is not in her vocabulary. She will be on to any ulterior motives, and she will not be taken in. Chances are, if you do not play it straight with her from the very beginning, she will toss you out of any possible future relationships. Do not try to dominate this woman, she is fiercely independent. She knows what she needs to be self-sufficient, and will go after it with unrelenting force.

Once this woman has decided to let you into her life, she will be a loyal, trustworthy, & reliable friend to the end. Like the Cancer female, she will respect your secrets and be extremely discreet. She will make great sacrifices for anyone who has earned her affection.

Do not try to pin any particular fashion style on this woman. She is undoubtedly versatile, favoring the passionate deep hues of reds, purples, and blacks. She opts for fast, sporty cars, again favoring the color black. If the woman stopped on the side of the road getting a speeding ticket is not an Aries female, it is more than likely a Scorpio.

As for this woman's home, her abode is generally a reflection of how she feels about herself. The higher her level of self-esteem the more care she will put into her surroundings.

More than most of any of the other signs, this woman is in to the mystical, and astrology often constitutes a favorite hobby. These women are often psychiatrists or spiritual healers. Whatever branch of work is chosen, study will not be difficult for the Scorpio. They like discipline and respond to it. All and all, this is a very complex woman that will enrich the lives of those around her.

PERSONAL PROFILE -- SCORPIO MALE

The Scorpio male is passionate, emotional and unpredictable. He is a fringe dweller, loving danger and challenge. He will confront any obstacle and fear no consequence. They are up for any adventure. He is seldom alone because of his dynamic, magnetic personality. A woman can feel a Scorpio man looking at her from across a smoky, crowded room. His sensuality and energy will not be denied.

The Scorpio male makes as ardent a friend as he does a lover. He can be understanding and compassionate and will understand your problems probably better than you understand them yourself.

Work is important to this man.. Although he is not high on physical labor, his intense powers of concentration and his vivid imagination, usually spells success. They make excellent detectives, policemen, soldiers, or big business executives. Because of their keen analytical powers, they can be excellent at predicting swings in the stock market.

As for hobbies, this man is drawn to heavy contact physical sports, such as hockey, boxing, soccer, or rugby. Many Olympic swimmers have been born under this sign, because aside from their love of the water, they are extremely competitive.

This is a very strong, exciting and confident man.

FAMOUS SCORPIOS

Hillary Clinton	Julia Roberts
Pablo Picasso	Bill Gates
Drake	Leonardo DiCaprio
Goldie Hawn	Ryan Gosling
Rachel McAdams	Katy Perry
Kris Jenner	Jimmy Kimmel
Emma Stone	Anne Hathaway

HERBS AND FOODS ASSOCIATED WITH SCORPIO

Garlic	Cumin
Onion	Lamb
Cayenne	Beef
Paprika	Olives
Cinnamon	

FLOWERS AND PLANTS

Red Geranium	Blackthorn
Rhododendron	Aloe
Honeysuckle	Witch Hazel
Catmint	

AROMATHERAPY

Jasmine, lemon, chamomile, lavender

SET THE TABLE AND BRING THE WINE

When inviting a Scorpio to your home, think of these words: intimate, exotic, unusual, and ethnic overtones.

Scorpios prefer a larger group of people, some of whom they know, and some who will be completely new to them. They like the comfort of the familiarity, but they also enjoy the challenge of analyzing new people. They will decide with whom they will speak to and for how long. Several Scorpios that were interviewed for this book suggested having a table of *small bites,* consisting of spicy pickles and cheeses, curried canapés, and spicy chicken wings. They love spicy, pungent flavors, their favorite textures being crispy and crunchy. The food should ask the question, "I wonder what is in that"? Exotic smells should permeate the room.

As for seating, Scorpio people do not like to be confined, so allow them to pick up a plate and roam at will. The truth is, if they become interested in a conversation, they may never get to the main entrees, so make sure to keep extra appetizers available, not to mention a well-stocked bar. Spicy, Bloody Marys or a salty margarita are a couple of their favorite cocktails.

Keep the lights low, as they revel in dark, mysterious places. I would suggest rich, dark red table settings; a blood red velvet tablecloth would be absolutely perfect. If you want to add a flower arrangement, I would suggest short cut red roses or geraniums. As for music, I would have some sultry blues playing in the background to really cement the mood of the room.

Here are some menu suggestions to arouse the passionate mood of your Scorpio guest.

This next dish is not for a faint palate. This shrimp packs a real punch to your taste buds. I would suggest serving this shrimp with a bucket of cold Mexican Lager.

Tequila Lime Shrimp

12 large shrimp; cleaned and deveined

1/8 cup tequila

2 tbsp. fresh lime juice

1 tsp. lime zest

¼ cup safflower or canola oil

¼ tsp. sea salt

Black cracked pepper

3 tbsp. butter

1 tbsp. oil

¼ tsp. red pepper flakes

Cilantro & lime wedges for garnish

Mix tequila, lime juice, zest, oil, salt & pepper in a sealable plastic bag. Add shrimp and refrigerate for 4 – 6 hours. Heat butter and oil in a heavy skillet. Pat shrimp dry and discard the marinade. Add pepper flakes and shrimp. Sauté until cooked; about 1 minute per side. Serve garnished with lime and cilantro.

Spicy Calamari w/ Tahini Dip

1 garlic clove; minced

pinch sea salt

½ cup tahini

2 tsp. fresh parsley

3 tbsp. fresh lemon juice

1/8 cup olive oil

1/8 cup sour cream

¼ cup grated cucumber; juice squeezed out

1 tsp. fresh dill

1 lb squid rings

1 cup mayonnaise

1 tsp. lemon juice

1 tbsp. hot sauce

Pinch of salt

2 cups panko

Oil for frying

In a food processor, blend, garlic, salt, tahini, parsley, lemon juice & olive oil until smooth. Stir in sour cream, cucumber and dill. Refrigerate at least 4 hours before serving. Combine mayonnaise, hot sauce and salt. Coat calamari in mayonnaise mixture. Next dip calamari in panko until well coated. Heat oil until hot and fry calamari until golden; about 2 minutes. Serve with tahini sauce on the side.

Tomato & Gorgonzola Salad

2 large beefsteak tomatoes: cored and cut in to 8 wedges

1 small red onion: peeled and thinly sliced

For gorgonzola dressing

½ cup mayonnaise

½ cup sour cream

1 tbsp. heavy cream

1 tsp. lemon juice

salt & pepper to taste

½ cup Gorgonzola cheese: crumbled

Mix together mayonnaise, sour cream, heavy cream, lemon juice, salt & pepper and half of gorgonzola together in medium size bowl. Refrigerate for at least 1 hour. Can be made the day ahead.

Arrange four tomato wedges in a wide circle on a decorative plate. Place a large dollop of the dressing in the middle of the wedges. Arrange the thinly sliced onion rounds on top of salad. Sprinkle remaining gorgonzola on top of salad. Can be garnished with fresh parsley.

Shakshuka is a very popular dish all throughout the Middle East. They say this dish originated in Tunisia, but all the countries in the region have adopted it as a mealtime go to. The pronunciation may vary country to country, but the essence of the dish has remained the same. Your Scorpio guest will appreciate the fragrant and pungent flavors of this meal. Don't be fooled by the eggs, Shakshuka is not JUST for breakfast.   It will be a hit at brunch and makes a perfect late night meal after a night out.

Shakshuka

2 tbsp. olive oil

1 small onion; diced

2 cloves garlic; minced

1 red, green or orange bell pepper

1 tsp. smoked paprika

½ tsp. ground cumin

½ tsp. ground coriander

Pinch of red pepper flakes

¼ tsp. sea salt

Black pepper

Pinch of sugar

1 28 oz can of crushed tomatoes

1 cup chopped spinach

2 – 4 eggs (depending on how hungry you are)

Handful of fresh cilantro

Crunchy bread or toast for dipping

In a heavy skillet, heat oil. Add onion, garlic & peppers and cook until wilted; about 3 minutes. Add paprika, cumin, coriander, pepper flakes, salt, pepper, sugar and crushed tomatoes. Cook over medium heat for at least 15 minutes so that the flavors have a chance to marry. Remove dish from heat and carefully make little "wells" in the sauce. Crack an egg in each of the wells. Cover pan and return to low heat. Cook for another 2 minutes or until eggs are cooked. Garnish with fresh cilantro. Serve right out of the pan with some crunchy bread or toast.

Bucatini all' Amatriciano

2 tbsp. olive oil

3 ounces thinly slices guanciale, pancetta or bacon

½ tsp. red pepper flakes

½ small onion; minced

2 cloves garlic; minced

1 can whole, Italian tomatoes in juice; crushed by hand

½ tsp. sea salt

Black pepper to taste

12 ounces bucatini or spaghetti

¼ cup grated parmesan or pecorino cheese

In a heavy skillet, heat oil. Add guanciale and sauté for about 3 minutes.   Add pepper flakes, onion, & garlic. Sauté until onions begin to soften; about 4 minutes. Add tomatoes, salt & pepper. Reduce heat and cook until sauce begins to thicken. Taste and adjust salt and pepper. Bring large pot of salted water to a boil and cook pasta until al dente; about 4 minutes. Drain pasta, reserving about ¼ cup cooking liquid. Add pasta and liquid to tomato sauce and toss over medium heat until pasta is well coated. Stir in cheese and serve immediately,

★ SAGITTARIUS ★

NOVEMBER 23 - DECEMBER 22
★ THE TRAVELLER ★

ELEMENT: FIRE
RULING PLANET: JUPITER
GEMSTONE: TANZANITE

PERSONAL PROFILE -- SAGITTARIUS FEMALE

This is the third fire sign of the zodiac, and like Aries and Leo, the Sagittarian shares their enthusiasm and a robust zest for life. As girls, they tend to be tomboys, but throughout life they will be good at games and athletics. They are the animal lovers of the zodiac and will usually have a pet; dogs and horses being their favorite. Many managers and volunteers at animal shelters are often found under this sign. Horseback riding is a favorite hobby.

This woman in naturally intelligent. She will not like restrictive discipline, and may not take to school in her younger years. She tends to be more interested in further education as she gets older. Once they begin to love learning, they become the eternal pupils, and all subjects will interest them.

The Sagittarius woman is very straightforward and honest; she tells it like it is. This can at first take some people aback, but you always know where you stand with this woman.

This subject is good natured and generous. She must have her freedom and travel is always on her mind. The thoughts of exotic, faraway places and uniqueness of other cultures fascinates her. You can always count on her to be in for a girls' weekend away.

This woman sums up the word independent, and she rebels against any laws, which restrict her personal freedom and privacy. Her sense of humor and outgoing good nature will give her a following of friends throughout her life.

Her clothing will always be informal. She would rather be in a pair of good fitting jeans than a business suit. But don't be fooled by her casual appearance, this lady can be all business and has the wherewithal to weather any storm that may arise. Eternal optimism is what keeps this woman buoyant, and gives her an unfaltering belief in the betterment of tomorrow. Like no one else, she always knows how to get the best out of today. This lady makes a great friend.

PERSONAL PROFILE -- SAGITTARIUS MALE

Like the female, the Sagittarius male will be careless in his youth, always looking for a sense of excitement, showing little regard for safety. To his credit, this man tends to learn from his mistakes, and he will eventually learn to develop his full intellectual potential. He will often be interested in philosophical studies, as he is very broad minded and optimistic.

Be ready for unpredictable behavior, as he is likely to show up at a dinner party in a sweater while everyone else is in formal attire. This lack of convention may mature in later years, but his conversational topics will remain focused throughout his life. Like the female, they will include sports, animals, and outdoor activities. We shouldn't leave out that languages are of particular interest to him, and because he will travel intensively, he often makes use of their study.

This male needs a great deal of exercise, both physical and intellectual. If he feels tired, it usually means that he is just bored.

It should be said for the Sagittarian mind, that once it is trained and disciplined, he is capable of a great deal. He tends to look at old problems from new angles, and is often able to breathe new life into a dying business or project. Again it is the enjoyment of the challenge that keeps him involved.

He will not be the worrying kind; in fact the danger is one of blind optimism, not realistically assessing the obstacles in his way. Some careers that attract this sign are attorney, veterinary surgeon, horse trainer, foreign correspondent, explorer, or sportsman. What this man cannot do is be restricted to a dull job in the office or on the factory floor. His ambitions must have positive outlets of expression.

As hobbies, he will take up strong physical exercise, sometimes in the form of extrovert sports, such as soccer or cross country cycling. They will often spend much time with animals, as they make no emotional demands. "A man's best friend is his dog", was more than likely a Sagittarian quote.

FAMOUS SAGITTARIANS

Taylor Swift	Brad Pitt
Myley Cyrus	Jay Z
Jamie Foxx	Katie Holmes
Chrissy Teigen	Chase McCord
Steven Spielberg	Julianne Moore
Britney Spears	Nicki Manaj

HERBS AND FOODS ASSOCIATED WITH SAGITTARIUS

Celery	Onions
Shallot	Ginger
Cinnamon	Chives
Currants	Grapefruit
Sage	Lime
Sultanas	Water Chestnut
Aniseed	Venison

FLOWERS AND PLANTS

Carnations	Borage
Balsam	Balm
Bilberry	Dock
Birch	Mulberry
Ash	Chestnut

AROMATHERAPY

Ylang ylang, rose, cinnamon

SET THE TABLE AND BRING THE WINE

As has been mentioned, Sagittarians do not take to formal attire or settings. They much prefer the informal cocktail party or outdoor barbeque where there can be lots of light chatter and physical movement. The Sagittarians interviewed for this book emphasized that they really don't care what you serve, as long as the host cares enough to prepare it. Some common denominators, however, were spicy appetizers such as chicken wings and lots of exotic finger foods. Like the Gemini, they used words such as unusual, different, new, and interesting to describe their foods of preference.

The truth is, these people are more interested in talking about the food than eating it. The social ambience dominates the tastes and textures of the entrees. Some suggestions may be to talk your way through the meal. You could pretend that you are traveling and take them through a cooking tour of the countries visited. An excellent idea would be to serve foods from a certain region, say the pastas and wines of Northern Italy, and while you are eating, take them through a descriptive tour of that area. Wine tasting would also interest this fire sign. Have wines from several different countries, and while they are sampling discuss the region and growing habits of each winery and pair the wine with an appropriate appetizer.

On an easier note, having well illustrated travel books on your coffee table will initiate discussion among your guests.

Whatever format you choose, be sure you give Sagittarians lots of company; they especially enjoy groups and conversation that flows.

Here are some menu plans to entertain your Sagittarian guests.

Beef Ribs Gochujang

1 tbsp. sesame oil

1 tsp. canola oil

½ cup green onion; minced

2 garlic cloves; minced

1 cup gochujang

¼ cup light brown sugar

3 tbsp. soy sauce

2 tbsp. rice wine vinegar

¾ cup water

In a small saucepan, heat oils and sauté onion and garlic.

Add remaining ingredients and bring to a low simmer; about 15 minutes. Set sauce aside. Can be made a day ahead.

1 cup soy sauce

½ cup mirin

½ cup brown sugar

3 garlic cloves; minced

1 2 lb. piece beef or pork rib

Mix soy sauce, mirin, brown sugar and garlic in a plastic bag. Add ribs and marinate 8 hours or overnight.

Heat oven to 350°

Remove ribs from marinade. Pat dry gently with a paper towel. Place on baking sheet and cook about 20 minutes. Brushes both sides of ribs with sauce and turn over and continue to cook for 15 minutes. Remove from oven and brush with a little more sauce.

Wings w/ Maytag Bleu Cheese Dip

1 cup mayonnaise

4 ounces Maytag blue cheese, crumbled (about 3/4 cup)

1/2 cup sour cream

1/4 cup buttermilk

2 tablespoons white wine vinegar

1 tablespoon lemon juice

Freshly cracked black pepper

Mix all ingredients and refrigerate for at least one hour.

2 pounds chicken wings ; split with tips removed

Preheat oven to 400°

Arrange wings on a baking sheet. Season with salt and pepper and roast until crispy; about 30 minutes. Check them in the oven periodically and move them around so that they cook evenly.

For the hot sauce

1 cup Frank's Red Hot or other bottled wing sauce

1 tablespoon butter

Red Pepper Flakes

Mix all ingredients in a sauce pan and bring to a simmering boil for 3 minutes. Pour hot sauce into a large bowl. Add wings and toss until they are evenly coated.

Transfer to a serving plate.   Serve with Maytag Bleu Cheese Dip and garnish with celery and carrot sticks.

This next dish will take your archer back to the opulent times of the Ottoman Empire when the great Sultans ruled the world. This dish is said to have first been prepared in the Imperial kitchen for Sultan Murad IV in the early 1600's.

Braised Lamb Over Silky Eggplant

(Sultan's Delight)

For Lamb

2 lb boneless lamb shoulder, trimmed and cut into 1-inch cubes

2 tablespoons unsalted butter

1 can crushed tomatoes

1 1/4 cups water

1 teaspoon sea salt

Pepper to taste

Silky Eggplant

3 tablespoons fresh lemon juice

1 large eggplant (1 1/2 lb)

3 tablespoons unsalted butter

3 tablespoons all-purpose flour

1 cup whole milk

3 tablespoons finely grated kasseri, pecorino fresco, or

semi hard sheep's-milk cheese

1 1/4 teaspoons sea salt

Braise lamb: Pat lamb dry and season with salt and pepper. Heat 1/2 tablespoon butter in a 4-quart heavy pot over moderately high heat then brown seasoned lamb, turning occasionally, about 6 minutes. Transfer to a plate and brown remaining lamb in same manner in 2 batches, adding more butter if necessary.

When third batch of lamb is browned, return rest of lamb with any juices to pot and add tomatoes, water, salt & pepper. Cook at a gentle simmer, covered, stirring occasionally, until meat is very tender, 2 1/2 to 3 hours. Season with salt and pepper.

Make eggplant purée while lamb is cooking: Prepare grill for cooking.

Fill a large bowl with cold water and add lemon juice.

Prick eggplant in several places with a skewer or toothpick (to prevent bursting). Grill eggplant, turning occasionally, until charred all over and tender inside, about 15 minutes. This can be done in the oven at 350° for 15 minutes. Remove from heat and cool slightly (eggplant will collapse), then peel with a sharp small knife while still warm, leaving stem intact. (This makes the eggplant easier to handle—it may fall apart otherwise.) Discard stem and chop eggplant flesh. Melt butter in a heavy skillet over moderate heat, then whisk in flour and cook, stirring constantly, until roux just begins to brown, about 2 minutes. Add milk in a steady stream and whisk until mixture begins to thicken; about 3 minutes. Add eggplant and mash with a fork or potato masher, until well blended. Stir in cheese, salt and season with pepper. Serve eggplant topped with braised lamb.

> **If you cannot find any bilberries, you can substitute blueberries, cranberries or blackberries. All of them work nicely with the following recipe.**

Venison Loin with Bilberry Sauce

1 2lb. venison loin (find this at any specialty store)

½ tsp. garlic powder

2 tsp. fresh rosemary; minced

2 tsp. fresh thyme; minced

1 tsp. ground black pepper

1 tbsp. sea salt

Combine garlic powder, rosemary, thyme, salt & pepper. Rub this mixture into the roast. Place venison in a shallow baking dish and cook for 30 minutes. Remove from oven and let meat rest for 10 minutes. Slice and serve with bilberry sauce.

Bilberry Sauce

½ cup butter

1 8oz jar red currant jelly

2 cups cranberry juice

1 cup dried bilberries

Place all ingredients in a heavy sauce pan and boil gently until sauce starts to thicken, about 20 minutes. Remove from heat and serve at room temperature. Can be made the day ahead.

The Astrological Kitchen by Angela Buck

CAPRICORN

★ ★

DECEMBER 22 - JANUARY 20

★ THE DIGNITARY ★

ELEMENT: EARTH

RULING PLANE: SATURN

GEMSTONE: GARNET

PERSONAL PROFILE -- CAPRICORN FEMALE

This is an earth sign, which makes this woman reliable, patient, and persevering. There is a strong sense of duty, and she allows very little to get in the way of this. Unfortunately, in doing so she may appear cold and impatient to others. The fact is, that she simply has no time for frivolous activity that the more light-hearted signs have. She is a highly organized achiever, and cannot respect a lazy person. In business she can become a workaholic who thinks little of vacation time.

This woman struggles with her ego. This tends to make her too self-critical and effacing, making it difficult to know when she has reached the top. When given a compliment, she will smile self-consciously, then point out the flaws of her work.

She is kind, faithful, and possesses an honesty that makes people want to stay near her. She makes a friend of long-standing who will be there in moments of need. She can be depended upon for her sincerity and support.

Like the fellow earth sign Virgo, her emotions are kept under tight control. This could be because she feels so frightened of having her feelings mocked. It then stands to reason that she must take the time to trust the friend or partner before her fears can be assuaged. She enjoys physical affection, but does not enjoy demonstrating it in public. She is considered the most proper of all the signs.

This woman needs a very strong man, sharing her serious overtones. She is too dignified for any of the more superficial signs. She needs a man she can respect, and whose faults she can laugh at. Her excellent sense of humor, in her mind, can only be shown in appropriate situations.

This woman is a conventional dresser. In the work place, she opts for the traditional blue business suit. Around the house, you are likely to find her in dress slacks, rather than blue jeans. Like the Virgo, this woman has a penchant for neatness and cleanliness. She is thorough and careful in donning her makeup, and enjoys feminine accessories.

In her home, she will show a lot of taste, accessories will all be in the traditional style such as marble fireplace and crystal vases. For furniture, she will go for quality far more than quantity. In the living room, there may be a few very expensive items, but you would be hard-pressed to find cheap & tacky adornments. As she grows older, she will work to make her home a delight to come home to, and it will gradually adopt the look of luxury.

PERSONAL PROFILE -- CAPRICORN MALE

Capricorn is the sign of the mountain goat; epitomizing the slow but sure climber in both politics and business. This Capricorn male will surely reach his goals in life if he has so aspired to do so. He is deliberate in his business and life decisions and always has his eye on the prize. Although this man may seem all work and no play, this is not the case. He enjoys his free time and likes to spend time with friends and family. One of his most delightful character traits is his sense of humor. His dry comments, if properly taken, can be very funny.

This man will be reliable, cautious, and able to bear hardships if life demands it. They tend to be conventional and the older males have found it difficult to associate with the permissiveness of the younger generations.

This man's mind is extremely rational, with constructive thought patterns. This makes him quite able to plan ahead in detail. He has often been thought of as *cool & calculating*. He has a plodding mind, and must work hard to grasp a new concept, but once he has mastered it, he will not forget it.

This man will not be attracted to any get rich-quick schemes. He believes in slow, steady progress, but he fully believes in the long term, he can make it to the top. He usually does.

In dress, this man is right at home in the traditional three-piece suit. They have no qualms about investing their hard earned money on the best quality clothing. They would rather have three good suits than six mediocre ones. Even on casual Fridays, you will find this goat in designer jeans, button down shirt and a well tailored blazer. He really is a class act!

The same philosophy pertains to the way this man decorates his home. Quality instead of quantity is a motto religiously lived by. He will gradually keep adding to his store of luxury items. By maturity, this man's home will be adorned with high-end furnishings and more than likely valuable artwork.

FAMOUS CAPRICORNS

Jim Carrey

Calvin Harris

Zayn Malik

Jeff Bezos

Bradley Cooper

Stephen Hawking

Kate Middleton

Betty White

Mohammad Ali

Mary J. Blige

Alfonse Capone

Liam Hemsworth

HERBS AND FOODS ASSOCIATED WITH CAPRICORN

Pasta

Beets

Malt

Potatoes

Corn meal/corn flour

Spinach

Quince

Barley

FLOWERS AND PLANTS

Ivy

Amaranths

Pine Tree

Poplar

Aspen

Heartsease

Pansy

Elm

AROMATHERAPY

Pine, sandalwood, rosemary, orange amber

SET THE TABLE AND BRING THE WINE

When entertaining Capricorn guests, it is vital to remember that they are oriented to a more formal setting. This would include a sit down dinner, with your best china, silver, and crystal. Bright, vivid, flower arrangements should serve as your centerpiece. Capricorns love rich food, extend your meal to at least a four courses. They like to dine well and in classy surroundings. If you are going to serve champagne, make sure

Breast of Duck w/ Lingonberry Sauce

1 duck breasts

Salt & pepper

¼ cup sugar

1 cup water

¼ cup chicken stock

1 tbsp. balsamic vinegar

½ cup fresh or frozen lingonberries

Preheat oven to 400°.

Pat duck dry and season with salt & pepper. Let meat come to room temperature; about 20 minutes. Heat a heavy skillet over medium high heat until hot. Place duck, skin down and cook until skin is brown; about 5 minutes. Spoon out the fat from the pan and turn duck over. Place in oven for about 12 minutes. Remove from oven and let rest for about 2 minutes. Slice duck and arrange on plate.

In a medium saucepan, bring sugar, water, stock, vinegar and half the lingonberries to a gentle boil. Simmer for 15 minutes. Pour sauce through a strainer and put back in the pot and bring back to a simmer. Mix cornstarch and water in a small cup and whisk in to the sauce until it thickens. Stir in remaining lingonberries. Remove from heat and stir in the butter. Pour over duck. Accompany this meal with creamy, mashed potatoes.

Roasted Beet & Goat Cheese Salad

2 medium sized beets

Salt

2 cups arugula

6 cherry tomatoes; cut in half

4 oz of goat cheese; crumbled

½ cup olive oil

¼ cup red wine vinegar

Pinch of salt

Fresh black pepper

½ tsp. Dijon mustard

Preheat oven 350° Wash beets and rub with salt. Place in oven proof baking dish and bake until tender; about 30 minutes. Remove from oven and let cool. Using gloves (or else your hands will be beet red) rub off skin.   Trim the ends off beets and slice beets into 2" pieces. Next, whisk together oil, vinegar, salt, pepper and mustard. Pour dressing over arugula and toss to coat. Arrange arugula on a salad plate. Arrange beets and cherry tomatoes over lettuce. Sprinkle goat cheese on top.

Pasta Bolognese

¼ cup olive oil

½ tsp. red pepper flakes

1 medium onion; minced

1 medium carrot; peeled & shredded

1 stock celery; minced

1 ½ tsp. sea salt

1 lb. ground beef

1 lb. ground pork

1 cup red wine

1 tbsp. tomato paste

2 28oz cans of crushed Italian plum tomatoes

2 bay leaves

½ tsp. black pepper

2 cups beef stock; warm

In a large Dutch oven, heat oil. Add pepper flakes, onion, carrot and celery. Cook until vegetables are soft; about 5 minutes. Add salt, beef and pork. Cook until meat is browned; about 10 minutes. Add wine and scrape bottom the pan with a wooden spoon. When the wine is almost all cooked off, stir in the tomato paste, crushed tomatoes, bay leaves and pepper. Bring sauce to a simmer and cook, uncovered for about 3 hours. As your sauce begins to "dry out" add a beef stock as needed.

When sauce is finished, toss with your favorite pasta, such as spaghetti, rigatoni, linguini or papardelle.

Medallions of Beef In a Peppercorn Sauce

1 tbsp. canola oil

2 6 oz filet minion

Salt & pepper

2 tbsp. green peppercorns; in brine drained

½ cup red wine

½ cup good quality beef stock

2 tbsp. sour cream or crème fraiche

1 tsp. cold butter

Soak peppercorn in red wine.

In a heavy skillet, heat oil, Season beef with salt and pepper. Add to pan and brown on both sides; 3 minutes per side for medium rare or 5 minutes per side for medium. Transfer steaks to plate and let rest. Meanwhile, in the same pan add wine and peppercorn and cook until most of the wine has cooked off. Add beef stock and cook until sauce begins to thicken; about 1 minute. Remove from heat and stir in sour cream. When the sauce is smooth, stir in cold butter until your sauce looks smooth and silky. Spoon over beef and serve immediately.

★ AQUARIUS ★
JANUARY 21 - FEBRUARY 18
★ THE INVENTOR ★

ELEMENT: AIR
RULING PLANE: URANUS
GEMSTONE: AMETHYST

PERSONAL PROFILE -- AQUARIUS FEMALE

This is an air sign, thus this woman lives on concepts and ideas, opposed to emotions and concrete facts. The Aquarius female is the most curious sign of the zodiac. She is always asking questions, simply because she just wants to know. The more out of the way and different the situation, the more she likes it. Her curiosity can scare off the more defensive types of people, but can delight those almost as curious as she is. She loves to be surrounded by people, especially if they have a lot of quirks and peculiar traits.

She is the best listener of the zodiac, and like the Gemini thrives on gossip, especially when it is entertaining and funny. Her alert mind and excellent memory allow her to have total recall of a conversation that took place a year ago. The Aquarian woman is a very friendly person who likes steady mental stimulation and excitement. She enjoys offbeat subjects such as magic and palmistry. Her original mind will look at things in a more reforming manner than other signs. Many inventors have been born under this sign.

In terms of romance, she will be detached and changeable. She tends to think of men more as friends than lovers, often leaving her suitors confused. When she does marry, she will be looking for a best friend as well as a lover.

In all relationships, the Aquarian must feel trusted, this is because she is highly trusting and worthy of trust herself. The seeking of truth is very important to her. If she finds out that her acquaintance or partner has been untruthful, unlike other signs that scream and yell, she will rationally try to get to the reason why. She is neither judgmental nor vindictive. She will analyze the problem until she can live with a suitable solution.

If communication with another does cease to exist, she will call the relationship over, but she will not feel devastated over this breakup. This is because she realizes the only stability in life, comes from herself; it does not depend on another. She is always looking for the creative and the new.

Like the Sagittarius, the Aquarius woman demands absolute freedom to come and go as she pleases, and she gives the same in return. Jealous partners make her feel suffocated and depressed. However, she does demand a mutual respect of privacy.

She appreciates the finer things in life, although her sense of practicality surprises many people. She will grab the restaurant tab the one-day, then turn around and order durable, medium quality furniture the next. She'll give her last dollar away to someone in need, as she truly believes in charity.

Because of her love of freedom, the Aquarian woman is most comfortable working on her own, often in her own home. She is the perfect entrepreneur, always coming up with new ideas and discoveries. Writing free-lance articles from her own home would also appeal to this woman. She would rather wake up in the morning feeling as though she will be doing something interesting that day, than routinely going in to a well-paid job. If she does work in business, it will be one where she works with a lot of people, and one that keeps her mind active.

Science labs, start-ups and the tech industry are a perfect fit for this woman.

As for her personal appearance, one may be taken by the striking clearness, often blueness of her eyes. She will accent her natural beauty with well-applied makeup and well-quaffed hair. She will be perfectly attired, having a leaning toward trendy and unusual clothing.

The Aquarian home will be well lit and modern. Since she enjoys constant company, and is always inviting friends and family to stay over, it is obvious that she would prefer a large, sprawling home with many bedrooms. If she had her choice, this woman's contemporary home would probably sport vaulted ceilings and light colored furnishings. She hates clutter.

When this woman is truly developed, she is a most powerful human being.

PERSONAL PROFILE -- AQUARIAN MALE

The Aquarius male is the true cerebral man. Being of a scientific and eccentric bent, he loves anything new: whether they be ideas, games, concepts, or technological innovations. They love to experiment with all of them, and then the next logical step is to see how to change them even further.

Before the Aquarius man can be affected by one's charm or attractiveness, he must be impressed by that person's intellect. He appreciates idiosyncrasies in others as much as he does his own. On a personal level, he is very idealistic, dispassionate, and humane. Because of his detachment, he won't allow himself to dwell on emotional snags long enough to bring him down. The first stab of sadness or emotional pain will apprise him that it is not really all that important in the big picture.

Aquarius is not a loner; he is openly interested in other people, as is happy to be involved in the lives of others. When a friend has a problem, he will cheerfully listen and then analytically seek an answer for the truth. He is curious and eager to help. In business affairs, he is not typically a hard, physical worker. If his creative juices lag, he may need to be revived from time to time. This must be done with tact and candor, for he will resist domination. He resents making explanations to anyone, and even a small misunderstanding can be blown from a molehill into a mountain. He can be highly emotional.

This man cannot deal with tradition well. Do not try to pin him down; he loves to travel and is happy go lucky. This makes it difficult for him to develop truly deep ties of friendship. He tends to know a lot of people on a lighter level. He is difficult to feel close to.

In romance, Aquarians have an uncanny knack for marrying their childhood sweethearts. In these cases they can be highly romantic and tender. If this relationship does not work out, it is possible they will spend many years, or the rest of their lives single. His home and clothing, like the female, will be modern, trendy, and in good taste. This male's home will contain every modern gadget known to man. They are reputed for their elaborate audio systems that dominate the decor of their homes. Expect to find the latest technology present in their house.

The metaphor that best suites this male is that life is just one big creative playground.

FAMOUS AQUARIANS

Justin Timberlake	Ellen DeGeneres
Jennifer Anniston	Oprah Winfrey
Amal Alamuddin	Christian Bale
Bob Marley	Michael Jordan
Abraham Lincoln	Ed Sheeran

HERBS AND FOODS ASSOCIATED WITH AQUARIUS

Dried Fruit	Star Fruit
All Citrus Fruit	Chilies
Allspice	Sumac
Wontons	Small, finger foods
Apples	Pears

FLOWERS AND PLANTS

Orchids	Solomon's Seal
Elderberry	Apple Blossom
Orange Blossom	Lime Tree

AROMATHERAPY

Neroli, lime, geranium

SET THE TABLE AND BRING THE WINE

The way to entertain Aquarians is very similar to that of the Sagittarian. They also like a lot of people in a party atmosphere, with music constantly in the background. They are more interested in talking about food than eating it -- it makes for intelligent dialogue. Both being restless spirits, the Aquarius male and female both like the idea of a table filled with appetizers, this way they can nibble on small bites and "work the room". If someone is boring them, they can simply just move.

Candles and incense are favorites, as well as the colors pink, gray, and different shades blue. Keep the setting informal, remembering that they do not like to be pinned down.

They enjoy a lot of finger food, as they do not thrive on very heavy meals. Seafood pates, emphasizing shrimp, are favorites, as well as fresh vegetables, favoring a ranch dip. Mild, curried dishes are another favorite, as are foods enhanced with soy sauce. Important to remember; the flavors must be spicy but not too hot. As for desserts, they do not have the proverbial sweet tooth. Although there are exceptions to every rule, most Aquarians would prefer a fresh fruit plate over a heavy torte or cake. The word with these people is light.

Cards and parlor games provide an excellent means of after dinner entertainment.

Here are some inventive recipes sure to please your Aquarius guests.

Aquarians love small plates or finger foods. They are more comfortable eating an assortment of appetizers instead of a large, heavy meal. These bite size crab cakes fit the bill. You can find lump meat crab in most grocery stores in the seafood section.

Crab Cakes w/ Cilantro Lime Dip

1 cup good quality mayonnaise

1 cup sour cream

Juice of 1 lime

½ tsp. lime zest

1 clove garlic; minced

Handful of fresh cilantro; minced

Pinch of salt

Combine all ingredients in a small bowl.Refrigerate for at least 4 hours before serving. Can be made a day ahead.

½ lb. crab meat; cleaned

2 tbsp. red pepper; minced

1 tsp. red chili pepper; seeded and minced

2 tbsp. mayonnaise

1 tsp. lemon juice

Pinch of salt

2 eggs; beaten

1 cup panko

Oil for frying

Mix together crab meat, red pepper, chili, mayonnaise, lemon juice and salt. Form into small, bite size "cakes". Dip the crab cakes in egg and roll in panko. In a heavy skillet, heat oil to very hot, but not smoking. Carefully add crab cakes and brown on both sides until golden; about 1 minute per side. Place on paper towel to absorb any oil. Serve with dip. Yumbo!

Soba Noodle & Shrimp Salad

8 medium size cooked shrimp

3 quarts water

8 oz package soba noodles

handful of sugar snap peas

½ red bell pepper: cut in strips

¼ cup sesame chili oil

1 tsp. rice wine vinegar

salt & pepper to taste

Bring water to a boil and cook noodles according to directions on package. Drain and rinse noodles. Toss noodles with remaining ingredients and refrigerate for at least 2 hours (can be made the day before). Garnish with fresh mint and lemon wedges when serving.

Empanadas are said to have originated in Spain, but have found themselves firmly steeped in all Latin cultures. In Cuba, these tasty little pies are stuffed with pork filling, in Argentina, beef & onion, and in Mexico, spicy chicken and sweet potato. Empanadas are so versatile, only your imagination limits what you can put inside them. Your Aquarian guest will love the curiosity of what's inside and the fact that it's bite-sized.

The Astrological Kitchen by Angela Buck

Chorizo Empanadas

24 empanada dough discs (these are found in all Latin markets and in many supermarkets in the frozen section)

1 tbsp. canola

1 large white onion; minced

½ pound chorizo sausage

1 clove garlic; minced

1 4 oz. can Ortega chilies; drained and

chopped 1cup mozzarella; shredded

Pinch of salt

2 eggs beaten + 1 tbsp. water

Preheat oven to 375°

Heat oil and sauté onions until translucent, transfer to mixing bowl. In same pan, sauté chorizo until brown. Add garlic, onions and chilies to pan and stir until all ingredients are well blended. Remove from heat and add cheese and salt. Arrange dough on your counter and place a spoonful of mixture in the center. Crimp edges to seal in mixture. Arrange on a baking sheet and brush on egg. Bake for 25 minutes or until golden brown.

Lamb Rib Chops w' Sumac Marinade

 4 lamb rib chops

¼ cup olive oil.

1 tsp. fresh lemon juice

½ tsp. sea salt

1 tbsp. dried sumac

Mix olive oil, lemon juice, salt and sumac together. Pour marinade of lamb chops, cover and refrigerate for at least 3 hours. Heat grill until very hot. Grill each side of lamb until desired doneness; about 4 minutes per side for medium rare and 5 minutes for medium. Serve immediately.

The Astrological Kitchen by Angela Buck

Orange Panna Cotta w/ Raspberry Sauce

Panna cotta

Vegetable oil

1 cup whole milk

1 cup whipping cream

1/2 vanilla bean, split lengthwise

5 tablespoons fresh orange juice

2 teaspoons unflavored gelatin

1/2 cup sugar

1 cup crème fraîche or sour cream

2 tablespoons grated orange peel

Sauce

3 cups frozen raspberries (about 12 ounces), thawed, drained, juices reserved

3 tablespoons (packed) golden brown sugar

3 tablespoons crème de cassis (black-currant-flavored liqueur; optional, but I highly recommend)

For panna cotta:

Lightly oil six 3/4-cup ramekins or custard cups. Mix milk and cream in heavy medium saucepan. Scrape in seeds from vanilla bean; add bean. Bring to a gentle simmer. Remove from heat. Cover; let steep 30 minutes. Remove vanilla bean.

Pour orange juice into small bowl; sprinkle gelatin over. Let stand until gelatin softens, about 10 minutes. Stir sugar and gelatin mixture into milk mixture. Stir over low heat just until sugar and gelatin dissolve, about 2 minutes. Remove from heat. Whisk in crème fraîche and orange peel. Divide among ramekins. Cover; chill until set, at least 6 hours or overnight.

To serve, spoon a little sauce on bottom of a dessert plate and then invert a panna cotta in the center of the plate. Garnish with an orange slice and sprig of mint.

★ PISCES ★
FEBRUARY 19 - MARCH 20
★ THE BELIEVER ★

ELEMENT: WATER
RULING PLANET: NEPTUNE
GEMSTONE: AQUAMARINE

PERSONAL PROFILE -- PISCES FEMALE

Not only is Pisces water sign, but it is also the last sign on the astral wheel. For this reason, it is strongly felt that the Pisces woman encompasses all of the best attributes from all the other signs. It gives her an instinctive ability to understand and empathize other's experiences.

This female is intensely feminine and insightful. She often feels that she is experiencing what others are feeling. Not easily deceived, she is able to see through to the real truth. Like the Scorpio woman, she cannot be fooled, but reacts on a less abrasive level. This woman avoids confrontation at all costs. Because of her strong sensitivity, she leans towards psychic ability. She could give psychic readings or therapy. On a lesser level, psychology or social work could give her a sense of purpose. On the extremist level, the Pisces could even become a monk or a guru.

In general, the vocation of the typical Piscean would be that of the artist, poet, musician, or dancer. Sometimes this woman is so talented she does not know what to do with herself.

Her appearance will be as feminine as her personality. She loves long flowing silks, fuzzy sweaters, and form fitting miniskirts -- anything to accent her sensuality. You will find her nails manicured, and her toenails polished. Her hair is usually long and flowing, with a dab of perfume on her tresses.

This woman may be the epitome of femininity but that doesn't mean that she does not have a mind of her own. She has many opinions and an independent streak.

Ideally, the Piscean woman's home is her sanctuary; it will probably be by the sea or other water source. Here, the melodic cacophony of the waves lulls her to sleep. This ultra-feminine woman likes to ornament her home with big, down-filled, over-sized furniture. This woman is known for her inherent good taste. There will be a lot of chenille and chintz, and a vase overflowing with freshly cut flowers. Soft hues of pale lavender, blues, greens and many tones of white will be prominent. Her kitchen will be spacious, housing a skylight to allow her herbal garden to flourish, kissed by the sun. She is generally a good cook and likes to experiment with different cuisines—finding culinary diversities fascinating. When this woman entertains, her guests always feel right at home. She has such an easy way about her – she doesn't judge—she accepts things and people as they are. Attending a dinner party of your Piscean host could be like lunching at the United Nations. She is friends or friendly with people from many walks of life. You could have a banker, musician, bartender and a priest all sitting around the same table! You just never know with a Pisces!

PERSONAL PROFILE -- PISCES MALE

Like the Aquarius, the Piscean man finds it difficult to be run by routine or schedules; he lives by his own rules. He inherently knows what is right for him and often lives in the moment. Pisces are one of the most creative and intuitive signs of the whole zodiac. He could spend hours (or maybe a lifetime) dreaming up new concepts or putting a fresh twist on an old idea. They will always give you an innovative and refreshing way of looking at the world. A Pisceans true calling is usually in the arts; whether it is theatre, television, publishing or animation. They always ignite our imaginations with their innovative perceptions on life and its inner workings. No matter what field he is in, he will choose someone at the top of that field to emulate. An example would be, an aspiring sculptor, would look to the works of Michelangelo. He needs to have a source of inspiration.

Pisces are freedom loving; spiritual individuals and their lifestyles must accord with this mantra. Pisces need a lot of room in which to dream, create, and enjoy their surroundings. If they are forced to conform to a life of a dull, humdrum routine—an unhappy life is sure to ensue.

Many men under this sign are self employed. If a Pisces does get caught in the net of "9-5", this could be palatable as long as there is a healthy mix of creative expression and flexibility at their workplace. For instance, working from home a day or two, or frequently taking clients out for lunch. A Pisces that spends a great deal of time working "on assignment" would suit them just fine.

Like his female counterpart, the Pisces male can be recognized by his dreamy eyes -- often limpid, usually large. His hair is often thick and flowing and usually sports an impish grin. Some people may mistake this man for being stand-offish, he isn't, he is usually painfully shy and keeps to himself. Once you get to know this man however, you will find that he is warm and open. He really would give you the shirt off his back. Along with Sagittarius & Aquarius males, this man loves the underdog and is always championing their causes.

Whatever choice of style they choose, it will make its own fashion statement -- whether it is suspenders and a bow tie, or board shorts & a t-shirt, remember they need to relate their clothes with their personal identity. No matter what he is wearing, chances are that he smells great! Their ever-present fragrance, usually with flowery undertones makes this man smell irresistible!

This male's abode will strongly resemble the female Piscean's, as they share the same sensuality and love of the water. If he is a bachelor, he may settle for a beach cottage, aptly appointed with big, comfortable furniture. It will most certainly exude a warm & cozy atmosphere. The Pisces male loves music. You may find him listening to melodic love songs that keep him in his own private world.

This man is an incurable romantic.

FAMOUS PISCES

Queen Latifah	Rihanna
Justin Beiber	Carrie Underwood
Eva Mendes	Daniel Craig
Jennifer Love Hewitt	Rachel Weisz
Adam Levine	Chris Martin
Cindy Crawford	Jon Bon Jovi
Jessica Biel	Steve Jobs

HERBS AND FOODS ASSOCIATED WITH PISCES

Seafood	Cucumber
Watermelon	Raspberries
Lime	Pumpkin
Lettuce	Sprouts
Chicory	Coffee

FLOWERS AND PLANTS

Water lily	Moss
Zinnia	Fig Tree
Hydrangea	Pussy Willow

AROMATHERAPY

Cedar wood, orange blossom, lavender, jasmine

SET THE TABLE AND BRING THE WINE

When entertaining a Pisces, keep the mood soft and romantic. The lights should be dimmed with the indirect light provided by candles, lots of them, in different shapes and sizes all throughout the room. There should be soft music playing in the background. Pisceans prefer a sit-down dinner, not necessarily formal, but with a plethora of cloth napkins in assorted shades

The Astrological Kitchen by Angela Buck

of lavender and sea green. They will appreciate fresh cut flowers as the center piece, I would recommend lavender hydrangea or water lilies floating in tiny bowls of water.

They are not the most punctual of people, so do not give an exact time when you invite them. These people are nocturnal, so a late dinner is more apropos. Because many Pisceans are in the theatre, yours could be a post-show dinner party.

Keep plenty of wines & spirits on hand; Pisces like to indulge in a nip or two. I would suggest also serving an after dinner coffee and liqueur as well.

With all of this on the go, it would be hard to go wrong. Enjoy!

Here are some dreamy menus sure to put your Piscean company at ease.

Cioppino is an American west coast version of the French classic seafood soup, bouillabaisse. This soup was created in San Francisco and has developed into a wildly popular restaurant offering. Since this soup is so versatile, you can add any type of seafood you want. Feel free to experiment with the seafood, such as king crab legs, squid, scallops and just about any firm, white fish, such as pollock, cod, Maui Maui or halibut.

Cioppino

2 tbsp. olive oil

2 tbsp. unsalted butter

2 garlic cloves; minced

¼ cup onion; minced

¼ cup fennel; sliced thin

1 celery stock; minced

½ tsp. sea salt

Cracked, black pepper to taste

½ tsp. red pepper flakes

1 tsp. dried oregano

1 tbsp. tomato paste

1 cup white wine

2 bay leaves

1 15oz can crushed tomatoes

1 8 oz. bottle clam juice

2 cups seafood stock

1 pound littleneck clams

6 large shrimp; cleaned and deveined

12 mussels; cleaned

½ lb. skinless, firm white fish

4 cooked crab claws; meat removed

In a large Dutch oven, heat oil and butter until bubbling. Add garlic, onion, fennel and celery. Sauté until vegetable begin to wilt; about 3 minutes. Season with salt, pepper, pepper flakes and oregano. Stir in tomato paste, white wine, bay leaves, crushed tomatoes, clam juice & seafood stock. Bring to a mild simmer and cook for about 20 minutes. Add, clams, shrimp, mussels and white fish and simmer gently until clams and mussels open; about 4 minutes. Add cook crab claws and simmer until they are warmed through; about 2 minutes. Ladle into serving bowl, making sure to put the same amount of seafood into each bowl. Serve with crunchy bread.

Grilled Halibut w/ Mango, Strawberry & Cucumber Salsa

2 halibut filets (you can use cod)

Salt & pepper to taste

1 tbsp. lime juice

1/8 olive oil

Whisk lime juice, oil, salt & pepper together in a glass bowl. Place fish in bowl, turning to coat. Let stand at room temperature for 10 minutes.

1 small mango; peeled and diced

3 strawberries; husked and sliced

1 small cucumber; peeled, seeded and diced

½ red pepper; diced

2 tbsp. red onion; diced

¼ tsp. sea salt

2 tbsp. lime juice

1 tbsp. honey

2 tbsp. chipotle pepper; minced

¼ cup cilantro; chopped

Mix mango, strawberries, cucumber, pepper and red onion in a bowl. Next, whisk together salt, pepper, lime juice, honey and chipotle pepper. Pour dressing over mango salsa and stir well. Add cilantro and stir again. Refrigerate until use.

Place filets on a very hot grill and cook until done; about 3 minutes per side. If you do not have a grill, you can broil the filets in the oven. Transfer fish to serving dishes and top with salsa. Garnish with lime wedges.

If you don't have the time to make the ravioli from scratch, don't worry. There are many high quality and delicious readymade pumpkin ravioli on the market. All you need to do is brown some butter and you have an impressive entrée.

Pumpkin Ravioli w/ Sage Butter & Walnuts

1 sugar pumpkin; cut in half, seeds removed

¼ cup brown sugar

1 egg; slightly beaten

¼ tsp.sea salt

black pepper

1 tsp. freshly grated nutmeg

2 pounds of fresh lasagna sheets

Flour for dusting

¼ cup salted butter

8 sage leaves; torn

1/8 cup walnuts (optional)

Preheat oven to 350°.

Rub cut side of the pumpkin with brown sugar. Place cut side up on a baking sheet and bake until soft; about 40 minutes. Scoop out pumpkin flesh place in a food processor along with, egg, salt & pepper and nutmeg. Blend until smooth. Sprinkle a little flour on a clean work surface and lay out pasta sheets. Drop a spoonful of pumpkin mixture on the pasta every few inches. Brush edges with a little water and place a pasta sheets on top. Cut pasta with a ravioli stamp or sharp knife. Seal edges.

In a heavy skillet, add butter and continue to cook over medium low heat until butter browns. Make sure that the heat isn't too high, or the butter will burn. When the butter begins to brown add walnuts and sage leaves.. Turn off heat.

Boil a large pot of salted water. Cook ravioli until done; about 3 minutes. Add ravioli and about 3 tbsp. of cooking liquid to butter and walnuts. Turn on heat to medium and toss the pasta in butter for about 1 minute. Serve immediately.

Cappuccino Mousse

1 cup cold whole milk

¾ cup cold, strong coffee or espresso

1 package vanilla instant pudding

¼ cup sugar

2 cups heavy cream

Whisk together milk, coffee and pudding mix until it begins to set. In a separate bowl, whisk together sugar and heavy cream until stiff peaks form; about 5 minutes. Fold heavy cream into coffee cream until well blended. Divide into serving cups and refrigerate or at least 4 hours before serving. Can be made the day ahead. You can garnish with whip cream and coffee beans if so desired.

FREELANCE GRAPHIC DESIGN & ILLUSTRATION

www.spiritdragondesign.com

✉ roxanneloncar@gmail.com

CPSIA information can be obtained
at www.ICGtesting.com
Printed in the USA
LVHW070004141220
674103LV00002B/6